Socialism . . .

Seriously

Socialism
. . . seriously

A Brief Guide to Human Liberation

Danny Katch

Haymarket Books
Chicago, Illinois

Haymarket Books
P.O. Box 180165
Chicago, IL 60618
773-583-7884
info@haymarketbooks.org
www.haymarketbooks.org

ISBN: 978-1-60846-515-6

Trade distribution:
In the US, Consortium Book Sales and Distribution, www.cbsd.com
In the UK, Turnaround Publisher Services, www.turnaround-uk.com
In Canada, Publishers Group Canada, www.pgcbooks.ca
All other countries, Publishers Group Worldwide, www.pgw.com

Cover design by Ragina Johnson.

This book was published with the generous support of Lannan Foundation
and the Wallace Action Fund.

Printed in Canada by union labor.

Library of Congress Cataloging in Publication data is available.

10 9 8 7 6 5 4 3 2

Contents

Introduction

Socialism is a good idea, but
> . . . it doesn't work in practice.
> . . . human beings are too greedy for it to succeed.
> . . . the rich and powerful will never allow it.

Most of us have heard one of these declarations in school, on television, around the dinner table. Whatever the specific reason, the lesson we are meant to take away is that socialism ain't gonna happen. Interestingly, the argument always begins with the reluctant concession that socialism is, in fact, a good idea. There's even a right-wing bumper sticker that goes a step further than *good* and reads: "Socialism . . . A Great Idea until You Run Out of Other People's Money." I realize that the guy with this message on his vehicle alongside Confederate flags and various other "I'm an asshole" signifiers doesn't mean it as a compliment. But it says something that even the most hostile opponents of socialism often start out by admitting that it sure sounds nice.

Perhaps they do so because the inverse is so obviously true. Capitalism is a bad idea. Imagine if we start a society on an uninhabited tropical island, and I propose that the people who do all the work will be paid as little as possible while the people who don't do anything but own stocks will have more money than they could possibly spend in their lifetimes. You would all be looking at each other and shaking your heads. "Wait, wait, hear me out," I might say. "We'll also treat air, water, plants, minerals, and other animals as objects to be exploited even more ruthlessly than workers!" Now you'd slowly back away because there's obviously something not right with me, even as I continue on: "Wait, don't go! We can maintain peace by creating massively destructive weapons and violent prisons. Why is everybody leaving?"

In this most capitalist of countries, growing numbers are concluding that capitalism doesn't work. Some of them have read sharp critics of the system like Noam Chomsky and Naomi Klein. Others have just lived in this world with open eyes and hearts. This is a positive step forward from the political climate in recent decades, in which critics of capitalism were too marginal to even be considered dangerous. But it's not enough to know what we're against. If we're not for something different, we're just daydreaming—or whining, if your personality is more like mine. Capitalism isn't going to collapse from criticism alone. People have cursed and denounced this thing for centuries and it's very good at deflecting opposition with a big "but" of its own:

Capitalism is a bad idea, but

. . . it's the only system that works.

. . . it fits with humanity's greedy nature.

. . . don't waste your life trying to change it.

One of the last major social systems to be permanently overturned was based on plantation slavery. A key turning point took place when the slaves of Saint-Domingue defeated armies from France and Spain to create the nation of Haiti in 1810. For hundreds of years before the Haitian Revolution, enslaved Africans had understood the injustice of this system and had fought rebellions to try to escape it. But after Haiti, these rebellions—from Brazil to Virginia—became revolutions attempting not to escape slavery but to end it. There is no socialist equivalent to the Haitian example to prove to the world that capitalism is no longer necessary, and books are no substitute for revolutions. My more modest aim is to introduce some of today's daydreamers and whiners to a concept that the world desperately needs.

What is socialism? I can't just give that away on page ix. What kind of an author do you think I am? Okay, fine. A short answer is that socialism is a society whose top priority is meeting all of its people's needs—ranging from food, shelter, and health care to art, culture, and companionship. In contrast, capitalism only cares about any of that basic human necessity stuff to the extent that money can be made off it.

Socialism is both more rational and moral than capitalism, but the question has always been if it is practical and attainable. That requires a longer answer. My pitch for you to read the rest of this book is that it will introduce you to the different aspects of socialism—its analysis of capitalism, theories about what a different world can look like, strategies for how to get there, and a history of movements, parties, and revolutions. All in a little over a hundred pages, which is barely longer than the "Terms and Conditions" you have to approve before upgrading iTunes. Unlike Apple, I want you to actually read the following pages because I'm not trying to trick you into signing away whatever rights to privacy you have left. That's just one of the many supposed crimes of socialism that capitalism perfected long ago.

If you do keep reading, you'll probably have questions about some sections and disagreements with others. I'll make suggestions in some footnotes and the main text about other books you can read that go much deeper than this one into various topics. You might want to learn more about the Haitian Revolution, for example, which for some mysterious reason is overlooked by the educational system of this country that was built by slaves. The best place to start is *The Black Jacobins*, an inspiring and beautifully written account by the brilliant Trinidadian socialist, C. L. R. James. Please read those footnotes, by the way, as they contain not just book recommendations but also silly tangents, hilarious jokes, and—in our very first footnote—a helpful tip on where to find the tastiest $30 artisanal free-range turkey burgers.[1]

Finally, a word about my tone, which can seem unusually light-hearted for a book about overthrowing capitalism: It's possible that there hasn't been a socialist book with this many jokes since Vladimir Lenin's little-known *Big Bathroom Book of Bolshevik Humor*.[2] The wisecracks aren't just sugar to help the political medicine go down—they're part of the politics. Capitalism is destructive and inhuman, but it's also silly, and mocking its absurdities reminds us that a system this dumb can't possibly be indestructible.

Those of us criticizing capitalism should be able to make fun of ourselves as well. Politicians can dress up every two-bit proposal about corporate tax breaks with big ideas about freedom and liberty—let the radicals who actually have big ideas put them out with a humility and humor befitting those whose dreams still far outpace our accomplishments. Jokes are also a safety precaution against the relentless negativity that is an occupational hazard for activists who spend their lives organizing against war, poverty, and other horrors that most peo-

---

1. In hell. (Hilarious joke number one! I'll be down here all book.)

2. Sample joke: "How many Cossacks does it take to screw in a light bulb? Answer: None, because Tsar Nicholas II refuses to invest in the countryside and as a result most rural villages lack electricity." It was funny at the time.

ple try to avoid contemplating for too long. We're looking for a positive path for humanity, not just trying to add to the chorus of news cranks and internet trolls.

Later to the haters. Socialism is for lovers.

Part 1:

Why Do You Ask?

1.

Ghost Stories

A ghost is haunting the United States—the ghost of socialism. All the old powers are united in their aim to eliminate this demon: Presidents and preachers, Hillary and Rush, Wall Street CEOs, and NSA spies.

Where is the Republican who doesn't claim that his Democratic opponent is a socialist? Where is the Democrat who doesn't run away screaming from this horrible accusation?

This means two things:

1. Socialism is widely seen by the One Percent as a threat to its rule.

2. It's about time that socialists should openly make our case to the world and replace the boogeyman version of socialism with a declaration of what we're really all about.

Did you like that bold introduction? I stole it from Karl Marx and Friedrich Engels. They won't mind—we're all comrades. Here are the opening lines of their *Communist Manifesto*:

> A spectre is haunting Europe—the spectre of communism. All the powers of old Europe have entered into a holy alliance to exorcise

this spectre: Pope and Tsar, Metternich and Guizot, French Radicals and German police-spies.

Where is the party in opposition that has not been decried as communistic by its opponents in power? Where is the opposition that has not hurled back the branding reproach of communism, against the more advanced opposition parties, as well as against its reactionary adversaries?

Two things result from this fact:

I. Communism is already acknowledged by all European powers to be itself a power.

II. It is high time that Communists should openly, in the face of the whole world, publish their views, their aims, their tendencies, and meet this nursery tale of the Spectre of Communism with a manifesto of the party itself.

The Communist Manifesto might be the most influential book in the history of the world, if you don't count the ones about God or teenage wizards. Within months of its publication in 1848, revolutions broke out across Europe. Terrified elites thought that the two young authors must have immense powers, either to prophesy uprisings or to create them. In fact, Marx and Engels had no idea that 1848 would become a historic year, but they did know change was in the air because they had been spending a lot of time with pissed-off workers, which was and still is an unusual habit for intellectuals.

People in Paris, Berlin, and elsewhere didn't rise up that year because Karl Marx told them to. But after they had taken to the streets, the *Manifesto* provided some of them with a vision about what their revolt—and future ones—could achieve. This has been the aim of socialism ever since: to demonstrate how the courage and creativity that people already possess can point the way toward a different society that will be built on those qualities rather than be threatened by them.

The United States in 2014 is a long ways away from 1848 Paris. I don't expect the publication of this book to trigger another American Revolution (although, wow, that would be great for sales). Yet the opening words of the *Manifesto* still resonate because we too are haunted. Unlike the European upper crust that Marx taunted for being frightened of a socialist future, today it's ordinary people who are scared of the future that capitalism seems to promise.

It would be one thing if the world had a lot of problems but things looked brighter on the horizon. People can put up with almost anything if they think that someday their kids won't have to. Besides, who doesn't like a good fixer-upper project? But the scary part about the past few decades is that things are clearly getting worse. According to the global charity Oxfam, the eighty-five richest people in the world have as much wealth as the poorer half of the world's population. Put another way, each of those fuckers owns as much as forty-one million other human beings, which is more than the population of a midsize country. The cruelest kings in history could never have dreamed of this level of greed—one man can only have so many fine tapestries and jewel-encrusted crowns!

In history class we were all taught the comforting doctrine of progress: Horrible things happened in the past, like slavery and the Black Death, but the world is now a more gentle and enlightened place. Yet it is in this world today that more than seven million people die from hunger each year, even though it has never been more obvious where to find the money that could save them. Then there is war. Growing up in the 1980s, I thought wars were bad things that countries used to do before they realized how idiotic they were. Needless to say I wasn't aware that even then the United States was involved in coups and covert military operations all around the world. But now we're back to straight-up old-fashioned wars that never end—in addition to coups and covert military operations all around the world. I could go on with examples of increased racism, sexism, and other supposed artifacts from the Bad Old Days, but most of you have the Internet. You see the same things I do: the police murders, the campus rapes, the vile comments at the end of the articles about the police murders and campus rapes.

The ultimate way to measure how we are moving in the wrong direction is with a thermometer. Global temperatures are rising, glaciers are melting, and coastal cities are flooding because of carbon emissions from oil, gas, and coal. That's bad enough, but what's worse is that the response of those in charge to the existential hole that humanity finds itself in has been to literally keep digging—for more fossil fuels. In 2014, the United States announced—in triumph instead of shame—that it had become the world's leading oil producer. The future of all life on this planet is losing to the short-term opportunity for a few people to make even more money. This fact alone should make the case against capitalism a no-brainer.

Declaring capitalism to be unfit to serve humanity, however, does not automatically prove that an alternative will be any better. In fact, it is commonly assumed that socialism has been proven a failure over the last century. Some of this is convenient propaganda for defenders of the status quo, but it is certainly true that neither the "communist" dictators of Russia and China nor the mild "socialist" reformers in Sweden and France succeeded in creating the liberated democratic societies that Marx and Engels described in the *Manifesto*.[1]

As a result, many people who are turning against capitalism do so with the assumption that socialism is also a dead end. But socialism is the only viable alternative to this society that anybody has

---

1. "Communism" and "socialism" used to mean the same thing in most contexts for Marx and that's how I treat them in this book. We'll get back to this question in chapter 9.

ever come up with, which means that anticapitalists who reject socialism are reduced to vaguely calling for the system to be replaced with . . . something better. This doctrine of "something better-ism" can unite people for a time against what they don't like, but it isn't so great at pointing a positive way forward.

Despite what you sometimes hear, young people today care about the world and protest as much as any previous generation. In the years since the banks crashed in 2008 there have been uprisings in country after country, from revolutions in Tunisia and Egypt to Occupy Wall Street and police brutality marches across the United States. The key difference between now and the sixties is not that our marches are smaller, but that they project less confidence that we can make a better world. As badly as capitalism is screwing things up, we are not sure that we could do a better job.

Therefore we are haunted—whether we know it or not—not only by the future horrors of capitalism but by the past failures of socialism. In one of his later books, Marx writes that the defeats of generations long dead weigh like a nightmare on the brains of the living.[2] Yes, that's right. Karl Marx even predicted the current glut of zombie movies.

And yet despite everything, socialism is making a comeback. Polls show that socialism is more popular than capitalism among some sections of the population, which is an incredible development. Even though many people would agree with Homer Simpson's memorable declaration that "in theory communism works—in theory," they can also plainly see that capitalism is not working—in reality.

---

2. The quote is from *The Eighteenth Brumaire of Louis Bonaparte* about the 1848 revolution in Paris. It's a tough read if you don't already know the history, but with some background information it's one of the sharpest and wittiest histories of a revolution you'll ever find.

But because few people have ever had the opportunity to learn what socialism means, much less be involved in a socialist organization, the word can mean almost anything to the left of slave labor camps.

Of course, this is in part due to the Republican habit of crying socialism at unemployment insurance, environmental regulations, and any other policy based on the idea that government programs should extend beyond bombing and jailing. I'm surprised some right-wing freedom lover hasn't yet held a press conference to declare traffic lights a Big Government conspiracy.[3]

As a result, the word *socialism* is in the air more than it has been in generations, but with very little content, a floating piece of pink crepe paper rather than a bright red flag at the head of a demonstration. It's more of a ghost today than it was in 1848. The aim of this book is to give this specter some flesh, starting with two simple but far-reaching concepts about socialism:

1.   Working people control the government.
2.   The government controls the economy.

Number 2 has been the main feature of countries that call themselves socialist or communist, but without Number 1—without democracy at every level of society—state control of the economy has nothing to do with socialism. Karl Marx, Vladimir Lenin, and Rosa Luxemburg were all freedom fighters living under kings and dictators. They were socialists because they concluded that full democracy was impossible under capitalism. By democracy, they

---

3. Sound bites from this imaginary press conference:

"Where does it say anything about traffic lights in the Constitution?"

"Don't tread on my treads!"

"I suppose it's a coincidence that the top light just happens to be red!"

didn't mean having a vote on one day in November, but taking an active part in all of society's important decisions.

Because we are so used to picturing the masters of both government and economy as narrow centralized powers that rule over us from a handful of buildings, it is hard for us to picture changes in society that go beyond replacing the people in those buildings with others who are hopefully more honest and noble. Socialism wouldn't just replace those people but the system that centralizes so much power in a few buildings. It would broaden the bases of decision-making to thousands of buildings and public squares and community centers. It is a system in which the people control the government by changing what government means.

Socialists first got a glimpse of this in the 1871 revolution known as the Paris Commune, which created a new form of government in which officials were paid no more than the average worker's wage and were immediately recallable if voters were unhappy with them. "Instead of deciding once in three years which member of the ruling class was to misrepresent them," Marx wrote, the Commune gave people the same ability as bosses to replace workers and managers when they weren't doing their jobs. "And it's well known that companies in matters of business generally know how to put the right man in the right place and if they make a mistake to redress it promptly."[4]

Just as democracy should exist beyond Election Day, it should also exist outside government buildings. Socialism is about giving people a say in how every aspect of their lives is run, which is not only noble but also more effective. Those of us who were lucky

---

4. The idea that companies always hire the right managers is obviously false. Funny how this isn't used against Marx more often by defenders of capitalism.

enough to observe and participate in Occupy Wall Street experienced a taste of this potential: committees sprang up overnight to create kitchens, libraries, beautiful art, and whatever projects anybody wanted to pursue, from supporting striking workers at Sotheby's auction house to challenging deportations in Queens and foreclosures in Brooklyn. One Occupier later wrote that "the skill and imagination on display mounted ever more as an indictment of the alienated world outside that kept us from sharing what we could do with each other, tricked us into selling our time and talents for money."[5]

One way to think about socialism is a society where there is no world outside of sharing our skills and imaginations. Imagine an Occupy Wall Street that is a thousand times larger and based in our workplaces and communities.[6] Occupy Health Care would be nurses, technicians and other medical staff, doctors, and patients taking over hospitals and clinics and deciding how they should be run. Occupy Our Food would bring together farmers, slaughterhouse and factory workers, and dieticians, ecologists, and vegans to debate out a safe, sustainable, ethnical, and enjoyable system for feeding ourselves. Soldiers on the front lines of this country's endless wars would form De-Occupy Everywhere and refuse to carry out any more deadly missions.[7]

This type of radical participatory democracy is the heart of the socialist vision. Long before there was Occupy, there were soviets.

---

5. This is from Nathan Schneider's "Thank You Anarchy." I'm less grateful than Schneider to anarchism, but I'll get into that in chapter 9.

6. Those who participated in Occupy Wall Street also know that we would have to imagine a version of the movement that created more effective structures for making democratic decisions.

7. If that sounds far-fetched to you, check out a book called *Soldiers in Revolt: GI Resistance During the Vietnam War* by David Cortright.

That's a word you may recognize from Russia's former official name—the Union of Soviet Socialist Republics—but you probably don't know that it means *workers' council*. Before it lost its socialist character and became a dictatorship, the Russian Revolution was led by democratically elected soviets. These local bodies sprang up in factories, military barracks, and peasant villages across the country to conduct the revolution in their local areas and elect delegates to the regional and national soviet government.

"No political body more sensitive and responsive to the popular will was ever invented," wrote the great socialist journalist John Reed.[8] As with the Paris Commune, delegates to the soviet could be voted out immediately by unhappy voters. Housewives, domestic servants, and other working people who didn't labor in factories could organize themselves into bodies and gain representation in the soviets. Only employers and police were excluded.

Soviets and similar bodies have popped up in many other revolutions in the past century, including in Spain in 1936. Here is how George Orwell described Barcelona that year in his thrilling *Homage to Catalonia*:

> Every shop and cafe had an inscription saying that it had been collectivized; even the bootblacks had been collectivized and their boxes painted red and black. Waiters and shop-walkers looked you in the face and treated you as an equal. Servile and even ceremonial forms of speech had temporarily disappeared. Nobody said "Señor" or "Don" or even "Usted"; everyone called everyone else "Comrade" or "Thou," and said "Salud!" instead of "Buenos

---

8. John Reed is played by Warren Beatty in the epic movie *Reds*. Sometimes I dream there's an epic socialist movie about me, but it always turns into a rom-com with a horrible name like *Guess Who's Commie to Dinner?* And I'm played by Zach Galifianakis.

dias." . . . And it was the aspect of the crowds that was the queer-
est thing of all. In outward appearance it was a town in which
the wealthy classes had practically ceased to exist. Except for a
small number of women and foreigners there were no "well-
dressed" people at all. Practically everyone wore rough working-
class clothes, or blue overalls or some variant of militia uniform.
All this was queer and moving. There was much in this that I did
not understand, in some ways I did not even like it, but I recognized it immediately as a state of affairs worth fighting for.

You may know George Orwell as the author of *1984* and *Ani-
mal Farm*, which are taught in many schools as antisocialist propaganda pieces. But Orwell himself was a socialist, who rejected
dictatorships that called themselves communist, but recognized and
supported the real thing when he saw it. The socialist revolutions in
Russia and Spain didn't last. Neither did Occupy Wall Street. But
that doesn't prove that the task of socialism is impossible any more
than the history of dozens of failed slave insurrections proved that
plantation slavery would never end.

Socialism may seem like a distant dream, and compared to our
current dismal reality, it certainly is. In country after country, with
the United States leading the way, working conditions and rights on
the job have been eroded. The term *working class* has gone from
being something that could inspire pride and fear (in bosses) to one
that evokes shame and pity. And there's been a corresponding change
in the idea of socialism from something that's created and run by
the workers to something that needs to be brought in by experts to
rescue them. But if socialism sometimes appears to be impossible,
we should take heart from the conservatives who think it's right
around the corner.

You can't go a week without hearing some Republican official
declare that the country is heading down the fiery road to socialist

damnation because it isn't letting enough poor people die of hunger in the streets. It's odd how many die-hard defenders of the free market in this most capitalist of countries seem to always have socialism on the brain, almost like a deeply repressed urge.

The sex columnist Dan Savage points out that so many antigay bigots have been eventually busted in same-sex trysts that at this point those who publicly denounce LBGT folks are practically advertising that there's a reason they are so preoccupied with sexuality. Could there be a similar dynamic at play with some of the most hysterical anticommunists? Is Glenn Beck going to be caught in a seedy motel room running an illicit book club about US imperialism?

But there is also some truth to conservative fears that all social welfare programs carry within them the dangerous germ of socialism. Not because socialism is about government control but because these programs are evidence that capitalism cannot meet some of society's most basic needs. One reason the right wing sees the specter of socialism everywhere—besides it being a cynical way to smear Democrats—is that they are instinctively aware that capitalism is a fundamentally unjust and exploitative system that is going to make people search for an alternative. In this paradoxical way, conservatives are often more attuned to capitalism's fragility than mainstream liberals.

In 2003, the Supreme Court finally overturned a Texas law that had criminalized gay sex, and the superconservative Justice Antonin Scalia was unhappy. Scalia warned that "if moral disapprobation of homosexual conduct is 'no legitimate state interest' for purposes of proscribing that conduct . . . what justification could there possibly be for denying the benefits of marriage to homosexual couples?" At the time, no states had legalized same-sex marriage, and many liberal commentators scoffed that Scalia was just trying to use scare tactics by raising the far-fetched prospect of gay people getting married. Of course Scalia turned out to be right, which is the only time I can ever remember that being a good thing.

Now that marriage equality is spreading across the country, some conservatives argue that it will undermine traditional gender roles, which many liberals dismiss as desperate alarmism. Instead, we should hope that it does. Enforced gender roles suck. From the time they are born, people should talk and dress and think the way that feels right to them, and not in accordance with some imaginary prehistoric chore wheel: Man = Hunt, Woman = Gather.

This is a good time to define what I mean by liberal, which is often used in the United States to simply mean anybody who isn't a Republican. Millions of people find themselves classified as liberals by default, ranging from those who march against banks and bombs to those who bail out the former and drop the latter. That's not a very useful category. One of the things I want to convince you of is that if you agree with the critique, the theory, and the vision put forward in this book, you're not a liberal but a socialist, and that those are two very different categories. Liberalism can agree with socialism that some things about capitalism should be reformed, and socialists often work alongside liberals to win those changes. Where we differ is that liberalism views reforms as ways to preserve capitalism while socialism sees them as steps toward replacing it.

Liberals have been pretty lacking for ideas for a long time. They've been able to skate by on simply making fun of how strange Republicans have become without offering any way forward themselves. But liberalism has its own more subtle form of irrationality. While Republicans are haunted by the specter of socialist barbarians at the gates, liberals mock their fears but ultimately believe that the existing system merely needs a few repairs here and there, even as society approaches ecological collapse and economic degradation.

Liberals deny the existence of ghosts—the pale hints of a world beyond the one we can see in our daily lives—because they lack imagination and are so constrained by what is "realistic" and "possible" that they can't grapple with the crying need for revolutionary change. Socialists have always known that specters are real. But some are more conquerable than others. The specter haunting right-wingers is capitalism's failed present and future, which they cannot remedy. The specter that haunts our side—the failures of socialism's past—is something we can understand and overcome. If we succeed in that, we can put socialism back on the agenda of the millions fighting for justice around the world.

We have nothing to lose but our nightmares.

2.

Dig Deeper

Polls conducted in recent years have found that almost a third of Americans[1] prefer socialism to capitalism. Breaking down the results, researchers found that socialism beat capitalism outright—49 percent to 46 percent—among people in their twenties and absolutely crushed it among African Americans (55 percent to 41 percent) and Latinos (44 percent to 32 percent) of all ages. Socialism also edged out capitalism (43 percent to 39 percent) among low-income people of all ages and races.[2]

---

1. I'd rather not call people from the United States *Americans*, which actually describes anyone in this hemisphere from Argentina to the Yukon, but no other single word does the trick. If you think I'm being "politically correct," imagine how people in France and Poland would react if Germany started calling itself Europe. I blame the Founding Fathers for having absolutely no imagination—just think, they could have named us the United States of Awesome. Maybe we should just count our blessings they didn't go with Slaveryland.

2. The polls were done by Pew, Rasmussen, and Gallup. Search "polls socialism capitalism" for details.

The media response to these polls is revealing. Coverage focused almost entirely on the results among young people, which prompted many articles about generation gaps and those crazy "millennials." By contrast, I couldn't find a single analysis outside the radical left press about the far more dramatic results among people of color. People of color are going to be a majority of this country by 2050, but those in power don't seem to give a shit about their opinions on how this place should be run. On the bright side, at least Blacks and Latinos were counted in distinct categories, unlike many other groups that might have unique perspectives about capitalism, such as folks with disabilities, Native Americans, or even that tiny segment of the US population known as women.

It also shouldn't be surprising that nobody in the media cared what poor people think about capitalism, even though there is a widespread assumption that low-income white folks in the middle of the country are almost all Republicans who put conservative values over their own economic self-interest. This has been a convenient myth for the Democrats, who often tell supporters that they sure would like to tax the rich and eliminate poverty but don't want to scare away less educated voters with such radical talk. (Speaking of the Republicans and Democrats, both parties have an average approval rate of about 40 percent, only a few percentage points higher than socialism. So why don't we have a Socialist third party? That's a long story and a subject for another book . . . which I wrote.[3])

What is more relevant for this book is the fact that these polls even happened. Until a few years ago, nobody asked Americans for their

---

3. *America's Got Democracy!*, which is available from HaymarketBooks.org and where all fine socialist humor ebooks are sold. I promise I won't try to sell you anything else for the rest of this book. Unless you're interested in a slightly used printer, in which case talk to me after you finish reading.

views on capitalism and socialism—not even the middle-class white ones! It's a remarkable thing to consider. Every day we are asked to "like" a product web page or stay on the line to complete a customer survey, but until recently no major polling organization had ever sought our opinion about the economic system that sets the terms for every decision we will ever make. Sometimes we're asked if we think the economy is improving or if president whoever has been good for the economy, but never whether we think this economy itself is rational.

This is less conspiracy than closed-mindedness. It probably never used to occur to pollsters to question capitalism, which would have made as much sense to them as polling anteaters about their opinion of ants. So what changed? That's no mystery. The great economic crisis of 2008 not only threw millions out of their homes, jobs, and colleges, but it did so in the most obviously unjust way imaginable. In case you've blocked it from your memory, here's a recap in four steps:

1. Financial institutions commit massive fraud that brings the world economy to a halt because not even the bankers know how much of their money is real and how much is fake.
2. The US government bails out the criminal banks with trillions of dollars.
3. The same government then doesn't help the millions facing layoffs, foreclosures, and student debt because of the recession caused by the banks.
4. During this process, George Bush is replaced in the White House by the very different Barack Obama, and yet almost nothing changes.

No piece of socialist propaganda could make the case any clearer. These four steps read like an IKEA instruction manual for how to assemble an unjust system. Inequality had been growing for decades—from 1979 the richest one-tenth of the One Percent saw their incomes quadruple while the number of people in poverty grew by fifty million. But that was a slow, mysterious process. In 2008 people saw the same thing happen within a few months, and it was obviously the result of a system that was stacked against us.

2008 was a glitch in the Matrix, a clue that all this time our supposedly fair and democratic system was an elaborate hologram. To switch metaphors, if we were all unwitting participants in a play called *Capitalism* about a world where people are rich or poor because they (or their ancestors) had earned that station in life, then in 2008 the back wall of the set fell down, revealing all the elaborate rigging equipment behind the scenes.

And yet the show must go on, so we continue to go to work and school as if nothing happened—but we can't erase what we saw. In millions of conversations in the last few years, someone has uttered these five words: "They bailed out the banks." The topic could be local school budget cuts or fast-food workers going on strike. The speaker could be seventeen or seventy, a longtime radical or someone who "hates politics."

This is the environment in which pollsters got the idea to find out what people think about capitalism. To even ask the question is somewhat to answer it. "Capitalism," Terry Eagleton writes in *Why Marx Was Right*, "is in trouble when people start talking about capitalism. It indicates that the system has ceased to be as natural as the air we breathe, and can be seen instead as the historically rather recent phenomenon that it is. Moreover, whatever was born can always die."[4]

---

4. Eagleton's book is a great follow-up for readers who like this book but would prefer one that is wittier, smarter, and better written.

It's been hard for capitalism to pass itself off as "natural" over these past few years. Banks like Goldman Sachs and JP Morgan Chase may have gotten away with crashing the world economy and still making a profit, but even they couldn't fool us into thinking that was in accordance with the laws of nature. Nobody looked at the massive government bailouts from Presidents Bush and Obama, took a deep, wondrous sigh, and thought, "Ahh, the circle of life."

Unfortunately, corporations also haven't forgotten about the bailouts, which taught them a terrible lesson: if you are "too big to fail," you can get away with literally anything. Unlike many people these days, I use the word *literally* literally. Consider the case of HSBC bank, which was caught laundering billions of dollars for Mexican drug cartels and groups linked to al-Qaeda. That is so villainous we can only assume that company board meetings took place in a secret lair inside a remote island volcano. And yet because HSBC was considered too big to fail (or jail), it got off with no criminal charges.[5] Think about that the next time you see the police throwing a Black kid up against a wall looking for drugs or read about a Muslim suspected of terrorism without any hard evidence.

What all this means is that even though the sharp crisis of 2008 and 2009 eventually faded, the "normal" capitalism that we've returned to isn't even the same place we were in—or if it is, we are seeing it with new eyes. It is a capitalism that has dispensed with even a pretense of justice or efficiency and openly operates on the principle that might makes right.

The bald-faced immorality goes far beyond bailouts. Because

---

5. Look it up. I promise that I am not exaggerating HSBC's crimes. They paid a $1.9 billion fine, which is huge, but only about five weeks' profits (not even income) for those assholes.

corporations have enough money to buy off politicians with what to them is just pocket change, most of them pay lower tax rates than someone making a salary of $40,000 a year.[6] Huge firms like Boeing and General Electric haven't paid a cent in taxes over the past five years—at a time when the government claims it can't possibly figure out where to find the money to keep bridges from collapsing, tuition to public universities from soaring, and food stamps from being cut.

Even the tech companies have lost their halos. Remember when Apple was idolized as a bohemian rebel, capable of making any product cool with a sleek design, a cute ad campaign, and a $200 price bump? Apple was supposed to be a new breed of business—an iCorp. Today it's widely seen as just another bunch of soulless suits who horribly exploit Chinese factory workers, produce junk products designed to break or be obsolete in three years, and set up bogus headquarters in countries with lower tax rates.

Capitalism is being widely questioned today because the past few years have shown that what is good for this thing called "the economy"—usually defined by stock prices and growth rates—doesn't have much to do with what is good for most of us. As the polls show, those with the most doubts are those who have gotten the rawest deal: African Americans have faced the highest rates of layoffs and foreclosures. Latinos have seen their communities broken up by the most deportations in the country's history. Poor people have endured cuts to every vital service, from public transportation to assistance heating their homes. Adding insult to injury, each of these groups has been scapegoated as freeloaders while the real leeches of taxpayer dollars remain above the clouds in their private jets.

---

6. Check out Citizens for Tax Justice for more details.

Capitalism deserves all the questioning it's getting, but we should make sure that the questions probe deep. When many people talk about capitalism, they are only thinking of its surface features: government policies that favor big business and the arrogant and selfish values of many business and political leaders. By the same token, socialism is assumed to simply mean a more generous society that allocates more resources to education, health care, and reducing poverty. That's a great start—don't get me wrong. But as the next section will explain, capitalism is a lot more than a few laws and attitudes that can be quickly reversed.

Here is a surface-level question: Should the government provide better unemployment benefits? Here are some deeper ones: Why is anybody unemployed who wants to work, given that this world has so much important work that needs doing? Why are employment decisions not based on what society needs but instead on whether businesses can profit? And finally: If anybody should face hunger in a society with so much food, why should it be the victims of that society and not the incompetent fools who are running it?

Questions like these dig way down to the rotting foundations of capitalism. Bring a flashlight and some thick boots. It's not going to be pretty.

Part 2:

Capitalism

3.

Welcome to the Jungle

Capitalism is supposedly the economic system most in sync with basic human instincts like competition and selfishness. It seems to me that if societies are based on aspects of human nature, it would be more logical and pleasant to build a new one around the love and laughter, but no, that's not what is meant. Capitalism fits the way we used to live when we were wild: dog-eat-dog, law of the jungle, and all that.

But dogs don't eat other dogs, and jungles have many laws, such as maintaining sustainable ecosystems and individual sacrifice for the good of the colony. How come capitalism doesn't involve any of that?

The whole civilization-as-jungle thing is a bizarre concept. Why did we spend the last ten thousand years discovering fire, painting on cave walls, developing writing, building Rome and Timbuktu, and creating philosophy and astronomy if the whole point was to eventually figure out how to live like we were back in the wild? And how could we possibly understand what laws jungles have when we are so busy chopping most of them down to build more Cinnabons?

Ever since the theory of evolution was laid out by Charles Darwin, it has been distorted into an illogical justification of capitalism known as "Social Darwinism." Evolutionary theory holds that species are constantly in the process of changing to better adapt to their environment—which itself is also constantly changing. Social Darwinists proclaim that nature favors the strong over the weak, and therefore the gross inequality of capitalism can never be changed.

You can't have it both ways. If capitalism is the result of evolution, which is dubious—after all, giraffes didn't evolve by writing economics textbooks arguing that longer necks will produce 50 percent greater leaf consumption—then it also follows that capitalism is not the perfect system that we have finally discovered for all time but one more phase of evolution that will eventually be replaced by something more suitable. Social Darwinists want to include certain aspects of evolution and leave out others. Just as plantation owners used to want their slaves to hear the Christian parts of the Bible about being meek and turning the other cheek but not the angry older Jewish parts about rising up against Pharaoh and escaping to freedom, today we are meant to read the book of Darwin right up until it gets to the present day and then slam the book shut and shout, "and everybody lived happily ever after—the end!" But there are still more pages in the book—hopefully.

Socialists are big fans of Darwin—not just because his natural history makes more sense than the Bible's six-day create-a-thon, but also because it is a wonderful illustration of dialectics, a philosophical approach based on change and contradiction. Dialectics stresses that things are both what they appear to be and a mess of conflicts underneath the surface that might eventually turn them into something else, sometimes over millennia and sometimes in an instant. A seed is a seed until one morning it is a plant. A population of apes evolves into a new species of early humans. Societies are also in a process of constant change, usually slow and barely detectable but sometimes explosive as conflicts beneath the surface come bursting out.

Capitalism emerged—slowly in some places, explosively in others—in parts of Europe from the 1300s to the 1700s. It came into being within the confines of feudal societies, which in their best-known form were dominated by large landowners who used peasants to grow food and knights to fight with other landowners. The internal conflict inside feudalism that eventually produced capitalism was between these landowners and a growing class of merchants who generated wealth through trade and investment. Merchants had been around for thousands of years, but these ones happened to live in a historical moment when Europe's conquest of the Americas and enslavement of Africans created unprecedented opportunities for wealth and power for those who weren't born into landowning families. This is how Marx put it in *Capital*:

> The discovery of gold and silver in America, the extirpation, en-
> slavement and entombment in mines of the aboriginal population,
> the beginning of the conquest and looting of the East Indies, the
> turning of Africa into a warren for the commercial hunting of black-
> skins, signalised the rosy dawn of the era of capitalist production.

As Marx's dark sarcasm indicates, capitalism exists today not because it is the best of all possible economic systems but because history happened to work out in a certain way—which included some of the greatest crimes in human history.[1] This fact by itself doesn't prove that capitalism has to go. But it does mean that the notion that capitalism came about "naturally" is either ignorant or, much worse,

---

1. And there would be more crimes to come: child labor, colonialism, sweatshops, Robin Thicke . . .

a justification of European (and Euro-American) tyranny over the world—as well as the tyranny within Europe of a small capitalist class. As an aside, this is why efforts to recognize the crimes of history—such as reparations for the descendants of slaves or renaming Columbus Day—are far from pointless exercises in "political correctness" about events in the distant past, as conservative critics claim, but an important part of understanding the world we live in today.

Of course capitalism isn't the only system that has seen horrible cruelties done to entire peoples. For crissakes, check out some of the things that God does in the Old Testament—and he's the good guy! But it's also not the case, as we are often led to believe, that human history before the modern era was just one long violent ignorant mess—minus a few heroic centuries in ancient Greece and Rome.

In fact, for most of our existence humans lived in small cooperative communities that some have called "primitive communism."[2] These are known today as "hunter-gatherer" societies, which had (and still have in a few cases) no classes or private property. These people weren't any nicer or gentler than we are today—clans waged bloody war with each other, although how often is a matter of debate. They shared resources because it made sense to do so in a society in which everyone in the clan depended on one another for survival and happiness. Hunter-gatherers were nomads who consumed only as much food and clothing as they needed because they had no permanent homes to store any surplus. The Enlightenment philosopher Thomas Hobbes famously described life in these types of societies as "nasty, brutish, and short." We now know that many

---

2. The word *primitive* has been misused against not-at-all primitive peoples to justify colonialism and slavery, but its literal definition—"early" or "untouched by civilization"—is accurate in this case.

of their lives were much longer than Hobbes supposed, and probably a lot less nasty than the lives of the poor in his England, which executed beggars for as little as stealing a few bird eggs.

Over thousands of years people learned how to domesticate plants and animals—in some places earlier than others—which gradually allowed them to produce more food than they needed and to store the surplus in case of future famine, which in turn led some people to stop being nomads and create settlements, which would eventually become towns and later civilizations. These developments, which are known together as the Neolithic Revolution, were both a historic advance and setback for humanity. They saved many from starvation during bad years and allowed for some people to be freed from daily toil to further develop our species's art, technology, and belief systems. But as more centuries passed they also led to a more ominous innovation: the beginnings of a distinct ruling elite.

The creation of societies divided into social classes happened gradually over the course of many generations. The specific features of class society differed widely in various parts of the world but a few broad generalizations are possible. At first a subtle distinction set the new ruling class apart—often they were respected elders tasked with the deciding how to allocate the surplus grain. As these elites became more removed from the rest of society over time, however, they created new traditions and institutions to make their dominance more permanent and secure. They developed a new category of property that was not communal but individually owned (or "private") to keep some of the surplus for themselves and the concept of personal inheritance to keep it within their families after they died.

Agriculture, private property, and inheritance led to a fourth development that Friedrich Engels called "a world historic defeat for the female sex." Having many children is more useful in an agricultural society where they can be extra hands in the fields than it is in a hunter-gatherer society where they are mostly extra mouths to feed. Thus, women's lives became primarily about having and raising children, which removed them from the status of being breadwinners (bread-growers, really) in the fields. On top of that, the tradition of inheritance increased the importance of being able to determine who was the father of each child. This led to women's sexual monogamy being strictly enforced in a way it didn't have to be for men, since it's usually pretty obvious who the mother is at childbirth.[3] And so began the development of the bullshit hypocritical morality around women's bodies and sexuality that exists in most cultures to this day.

These concepts of private property, inheritance, and women's subordination originated in the earliest ruling classes but eventually became accepted norms for all members of agricultural class societies—although of course the specific forms they took varied widely as human civilization spread and developed throughout the world. Over the past few thousand years many different types of societies came into being in which minority ruling classes have controlled the economic surpluses created by the masses and put them to different uses. In the ancient eras of Athens, Mexico, and Mali, small segments of the populace living off the labor of conquered slaves built astounding legacies of science, art, and philosophy. The lands that today are Germany and Japan saw feudal societies in which each wealthy landowner used the food and crafts created by his peasants to pay for elaborate castles and warriors to raid other wealthy landowners' castles.

It was out of these types of feudal societies in Europe that capitalism began to develop, first through merchants and wealthy

---

3. If you're not sure why this is, ask the kids at school to draw you some pictures.

craftsmen,[4] then through factory owners and bankers, and now through Oprah and Bono. Capitalism is by far the most productive and innovative class society because it is based not on land but on capital that can be reinvested, and on competition between capitalists, which forces them to take most of the capital created by their workers and invest it back into developing new methods of creating even more capital. This is why technology has developed much more in one capitalist decade than it did for entire centuries before the 1800s.[5] It's also why the European and North American countries that developed capitalism first gained an enormous advantage that enabled them to drag the rest of the world into their new system on quite unfavorable terms.

Capitalism has achieved amazing things, some of which are appreciated most of all by socialists, who aren't blinded by the Social Darwinist propaganda that this is humanity's natural state. It's in the first part of *The Communist Manifesto* that you'll find some of the most accurate praise of the capitalist class as "the first to show what man's activity can bring about. It has accomplished wonders far surpassing Egyptian pyramids, Roman aqueducts, and Gothic cathedrals." These wonders—from railroads to vaccines to space flight—promise a future of widespread abundance and leisure time. Unfortunately, that future has been around the corner for the past hundred years.

The problem is that while capitalism produces so much surplus that for the first time in history there is enough for every single person

---

4. Yes, craftsmen and not craftspeople. I never use man to refer to people and I apologize in advance for some people I quote in this book who do, as Marx is about to in a few paragraphs.

5. The phenomenon of everybody over the age of thirty-five feeling hopelessly intimidated by the latest technology is a recent development. No farmer ever needed to ask his seven-year-old daughter "how to work this new-fangled steel plow thingy."

to live and live well, it still requires—as previous class societies did—that surplus to be controlled and guarded by a small minority, so that the rest of us have to go to work for them and create more capital. In other words, capitalism has created a world in which capitalists should now be obsolete.

For almost all of our species's history, our main problem has been not having enough: not enough food, fertile land, or drinkable water. Now we produce too much, which should be a cause for celebration but instead is a curse, because when capitalists overproduce they lose on their investment and lay off millions of workers. Our second-biggest problem used to be disease. Today we can produce and distribute vaccines and treatments for the most widespread illnesses around the world, such as malaria and AIDS, but we only do so for those who have the money to afford medicines and treatment. But you don't have to live in sub-Saharan Africa to experience the outmoded irrationality of capitalism. Just go online.

The Internet is the most important technological development of our lifetimes. And yet because it is a system of communication based on information, ideas, and art being instantly shared and collaboratively developed across the world, the main concern that capitalism has had with it is how to turn it into something that can be privately hoarded and sold. This process has been relatively smooth for some traditional businesses that have simply shifted their focus to online sales. But many of the biggest Internet sites are entirely based on content created and shared by users. Some, like Wikipedia and Craigslist, have embraced the noncapitalist model. But others like Google and Facebook spent years trying to figure out how to convert their usefulness into profit, until they finally found a way: by selling user information to advertisers who can now track our every online move.

It is common knowledge in the tech world that "if you're not paying for the product, you are the product." Google and Facebook are essentially spying on us every day, not because this was their sinister plan all along,[6] but because that was the only way capitalists could figure out how to make the Internet worth their investment. Decades ago comics like Yakov Smirnoff used to do "Russian Reversal" jokes: "In America you can always find a party! In Soviet Russia, party always finds you." Maybe somewhere today a comedian is working on her American Reversal routine: "In Capitalist America, Google searches you!" The transformation of these tech capitalists from a ragtag bunch of fairly anti-establishment computer geeks into creepy Orwellian overlords was not a "natural" process of evolution but a nonsensical path created by capitalist rules that no longer fit the environment that the Internet has created.

It's time to take charge of our own evolution and have the majority who create society's wealth control how it is distributed. We now have the ability to combine the egalitarianism and democracy of preclass societies with the material abundance and technological capability of twenty-first-century capitalism. We can realize the dream of all of humanity: being part of the same clan.

---

6. That would be our government. More on that in chapter 5.

4.

Freedom Isn't Free

If there is a Karl Marx of capitalism, it is probably Adam Smith, the Scottish philosopher and economist who in 1776 wrote *The Wealth of Nations*, which introduced the world to the concepts of the "free market" and the "invisible hand." Smith meant these to be metaphors that could help people understand the complicated workings of this new social order he was trying to describe, but his metaphors have been transformed over the centuries into gods that modern economists believe really exist and need to be worshipped and appeased. But we shouldn't blame Adam Smith for the stupidities of people who claim to be his disciples,[1] and before we get into the weaknesses in his theories it is worth appreciating their positive contributions.

Smith didn't invent capitalism. He observed it from his perch at the University of Glasgow, a Scottish city at the heart of the industrial revolution. Just a few generations before, most people in

---

1. The same is true for Marx, who disagreed so strongly with many of his followers that he once declared, "If anything is certain, it is that I myself am not a Marxist."

Scotland were peasants who farmed their own land, turned over part of their crop to their local lord, and kept whatever was left over to feed and clothe themselves. By Smith's time, economic activity was increasingly based on the trade among merchants and manufacturers. More people were spending their days producing one particular product and using their wages from this work to buy food and clothing produced by others. Ironically for someone known today for his embrace of cutthroat capitalism, one of the things Smith appreciated most about his changing society was how it brought all sorts of people together in a shared economic project. In a famous passage from *The Wealth of Nations*, he marvels at the collaborative nature of this new economy:

> The woolen coat, for example, which covers the day-labourer, as coarse and rough as it may appear, is the produce of the joint labour of a great multitude of workmen. The shepherd, the sorter of the wool, the wool-comber or carder, the dyer, the scribbler, the spinner, the weaver, the fuller, the dresser, with many others, must all join their different arts in order to complete even this homely production.
>
> How many merchants and carriers, besides, must have been employed in transporting the materials from some of those workmen to others who often live in a very distant part of the country! . . . how many ship-builders, sailors, sail-makers, rope-makers, must have been employed in order to bring together the different drugs made use of by the dyer, which often come from the remotest corners of the world! . . .
>
> [I]f we examine, I say, all these things, and consider what a variety of labour is employed about each of them, we shall be sensible that without the assistance and co-operation of many thousands, the very meanest person in a civilized country could not be provided, even according to, what we very falsely imagine, the easy and simple manner in which he is commonly accommodated.

This interconnectedness was only to increase over the next two centuries as capitalism spread to every corner of the globe, bringing horrors in its wake like sweatshops and pollution. Looking at this new system through Smith's eyes, however, reminds us of the beautiful aspects of the ways it has tied humanity together through millions of daily productive relationships. Marx and others would build on this part of Smith's vision. But we're not there yet. In 1776 the working class had barely begun to exist in a few cities like Glasgow. It would be another thirty years until it began taking large-scale strike actions and putting forward its own ideas about how the world should be run.

The people who grabbed Smith's attention were the capitalists, many of whom were his friends in Glasgow. This rising new class was starting to amass great wealth, but it was not the capitalist class in power that we know today. At the time Britain was still mostly ruled by the aristocratic landowning class, with its rigid feudal hierarchies based on whether you were born into the family of the Duke of Such and Such or the Earl of Whatever. In this context, *The Wealth of Nations* was a radical argument that the capitalist class had discovered a better way for society to be run.

This way was built upon three basic elements: self-interest, competition, and accumulation. Together these formed a potent synthesis: the first drives innovation, the second spreads the benefits of innovation across society, and the third produces more innovation. Self-interest leads a capitalist to invest in manufacturing woolen coats to make a profit. Competition from other coat manufacturers ensures that the capitalist cannot charge an "unfair" price. This competition also leads the coat maker to not simply pocket his profits but to accumulate them to reinvest in better machinery and new technology to get ahead of the other manufacturers.

All of this activity takes place in what Smith called the free market, which is not a real place but a way to understand the commercial realm in which buyers and sellers trade goods and services. They key word for Smith was *free*, meaning that these are voluntary transactions, unlike the obligatory relationships in previous societies between lords and peasants or slaves and slave owners. As socialist journalist Eric Ruder puts it:

> For the economists who defend capitalism, the free market itself is a realm of freedom and equality, evaluating and rewarding—or not rewarding—individuals' economic contributions on the basis of their worth. . . .
>
> Why this single-minded faith in the powers of the free market? It goes back to economist Adam Smith's 250-year-old proposition that the genius of the system is that exchanges in a capitalist free market are voluntary—we don't have to work for a certain company, we're not obligated to buy their products, they're not required to deal with other companies, and so on. . . .
>
> On the surface, the point seems legitimate. No one forces shoppers to buy a new toaster or an iPhone or an airline flight they don't want or need. But the market doesn't just facilitate exchanges between consumers and the corporations that produce the goods they buy. It also coordinates and regulates the exchange between capital and labor. In other words, the free market, with its mechanism of supply and demand, sets the rate at which workers are compensated. McDonald's may pay less than $10 an hour, but that's because there's a supply of workers willing to take jobs at that wage.[2]

In other words, Smith's theory is that the free market is, in the words of economist Robert Heilbroner, a "self-regulating system for

2. This is from Eric's article "Inequality and the Unfree Market" at SocialistWorker.org. There are many great articles at that site, and I'm only partly saying that because some of them are mine.

society's orderly provisioning." Smith referred to this self-regulating system as an "invisible hand" that directs the millions of exchanges between buyers and sellers of goods and labor toward their most efficient and productive use for society. Smith believed that capitalists' desire to make money and get ahead was a positive good for society, which has led many a modern executive to honor him as the patron saint of greed. But Smith was an intellectual, not a businessman—a true champion of freedom and individual rights at a time when society's most cherished values were obedience and not challenging the destiny into which you were born. Smith's point was that the economic choices of millions of merchants, manufacturers, workers, and consumers would create a more intelligent society than the edicts of even the noblest king. His argument that an economy based on unregulated trade and competition was better than one rigidly controlled by the monarchy was a progressive case for democracy.

The next two centuries were to prove him right. And wrong, since capitalism has led to more death and destruction than the most ruthless kings in history could ever have dreamed of causing: world wars, forced migrations across continents, and starvation in the midst of plenty. There have turned out to be some giant holes in Smith's theories.

Tyranny: Exploitation and Oppression

Most participants in the "free market" are actually not at all free. Why is it that there is such a large supply of workers who are willing—eager even—to work for low pay at McDonald's? Since many of us are or have been in that position ourselves, the answer is obvious: people have to take those jobs if they want to provide themselves or their families with the basic necessities. This means, as Ruder points out, that the decision to work for someone else—to sell our labor on the market—is only a voluntary or "free decision" for rich people who don't have to work in order to survive. The rest of us are forced to labor for others just as much as the peasants and slaves throughout history. The only freedom that a worker has under capitalism—and it's an important one—is that she doesn't have to toil for a particular lord or slave owner for the rest of her life but can bounce around working for many different bosses—sometimes by her choice and sometimes by theirs.

You might think that supporters of the "free market" would want to guarantee that everyone has access to decent health care, housing, food, and transportation so that workers would have the same freedom to sell—or not sell—their labor as the One Percent. Instead, such proposals are viewed as socialist because protections for workers such as minimum wage laws, unemployment insurance, and unions interfere with the workings of the free market. But attacking these programs gives workers even less freedom to decide whether or not to take or stay in a dead-end or abusive job. Clearly, the definition of freedom changes depending on which side of the counter you're standing on in the "free" market.

The irony of the free market concept is that capitalism would cease to function if most people had the true freedom of economic security. Nobody would work minimum wage jobs in fast food. In fact few people would work for anybody else, period—because to work for someone else under capitalism is to be exploited. All bosses—not just the mean ones—exploit their workers, by which I mean all bosses keep for themselves some of the value produced by workers. This theft is how businesses make profits.

Let's say I own a company that makes CDs for a music label that specializes in mashups of German house music and late nineties slow jams.[3] Not surprisingly, we're a very small business with only one employee: you. You make $25 an hour, or $200 for an eight-hour day. Each day we make (okay, you make) fifty CDs of *Bell Biv DeVolkswagen* that sell for $10 each, for a total of $500. (For the purposes of this example, we'll assume that every CD will be sold, although that's not how it works in the real world, as we'll get to later.) As a worker, you spend your days forced to listen to R. Kelley crooning over Bavarian electronica, acutely aware that you are receiving $25 for every hour that you don't run screaming out of the building.

As the owner, I look at your day quite differently. My daily expenses are $200 for your salary plus another $200 for rent, machinery, and other materials. From my perspective, the first twenty CDs you make—which take you a little over three hours—pay off your wages. The next twenty pay for my other expenses. Now that I've made my $400 back, the final part of your day when you make the last ten CDs belongs completely to me. I keep that final $100 as a profit on my $400 investment. Whether or not you're happy to be making $25 an hour, I have kept for myself some of the wealth that you created. If the business grows and I have ten employees, I'll be making $1,000 a day, "earning" that profit not by making the CDs—and certainly not by providing the world with good music— but simply because I had the capital in the first place to rent the space and buy the materials. And chances are, the reason you are the one doing the work and not seeing the profit is because you didn't.

This relationship between those who are forced to sell their labor and those who have the capital to use it to make a profit is what socialists call exploitation. All profits are based on exploitation, which is obvious to most people who have ever had a job, but also

---

3. Don't judge me. I'm entitled to outside interests.

tricky to prove. In the daily workings of capitalism, a company's profitability can depend on many changing factors, from the price of gas to current consumer tastes. This is supposed to be why we have a science called economics, since science can explain things that we can't figure out through everyday observation, like germs and evolution. Unfortunately, most of what we know as economics isn't based on scientific research into how capitalism works but propaganda promoting its wonders. You might think, for example, that economics textbooks would be interested in understanding the source of profits. After all, profit is the daily bread of capitalism, the first consideration in almost every major decision our society makes. Toothpaste manufacturers produce and market more than three hundred different types and sizes of toothpaste in the United States because doing so makes profits, and the health care system doesn't allow a hundred million Americans to visit the dentist each year because that would not make a profit. Your daughter is taking more standardized tests and doing more homework in the hopes this will one day make her a more productive and profit-generating worker, and your father's old factory has been moved a thousand miles to a rural area where it is hoped the workers will accept less pay and therefore the company will make more profits.

And yet most textbooks don't even devote a single chapter to the question of where profit comes from. Instead they take its existence for granted and move right on to concepts like supply and demand, and efficiency and elasticity, to explain what makes profits rise for one company or industry and fall for others. This may be all that matters from the perspective of capitalists, but it doesn't answer the question of what makes the total amount of society's capital grow larger, as it does every year except during recessions. In effect, mainstream economics deals with profits the way any of us would regard a bank account that mysteriously added an extra thousand dollars each month that we couldn't account for. We would certainly think a lot about what to do with that extra money, but we wouldn't ask too many questions about where it came from, suspecting that we probably don't want to know the answer.

When the question of profits is addressed in mainstream economics, it's not to figure out where they came from but to justify why they should go to bosses who often did little to earn them. Thus, many economists claim that profits are a reward given to capitalists for the risk of investing in a business. Somehow, according to this theory, the Invisible Hand that allocates resources based on supply and demand actually belongs to a jolly Invisible Uncle who likes to slip a little something extra to capitalists as a show of gratitude for their bravery. The most laughable part is the idea that it's rich people who are the major risk-takers in our society. If capitalism really awarded profits to those who took risks to add to the national wealth, bosses and investors would have to get far back in line behind construction workers, firefighters, and undocumented immigrants.

Defenders of capitalism reach for these and other outlandish theories because it's awkward to acknowledge that the real source of profit is the workers who don't see any of it. But if you're not in the business of apologizing for the system, you can actually recognize that there is some good news here. We are an intelligent and creative species that has figured out how to produce far more than we need to personally consume. This productivity should be fantastic news: no more hunger and homelessness, and no coming back to work after lunch!

But no, under capitalism workers don't get to decide what to do with the surplus they create. Instead that money goes into profits, which owners use partly on nice suits and luxury homes but mostly plow back into production—often to exploit us more or even replace us. Technological advancements that we are promised will make our jobs easier are used to exploit us further. That incredible new software program that you thought would save you some time entering data is now causing the person in the next cubicle to be laid off—and you're expected to pick up half his work.

Many workers are not exploited in the strict economic sense of the word because they don't work for a private company, but they have a similar relationship to capitalism. Government employees such as teachers, mail carriers, and highway workers don't produce profit for private companies, and their salaries come from taxes paid by the entire population. But the decisions about how, where, and for how much they do their jobs are still determined by the needs of business—specifically its desire to spend the least amount of tax dollars required to have an adequately educated labor force that can make it to work on time. Protests for more funding for schools and post offices are therefore fights over the use of capitalists' profits, just as much as strikes in corporate-owned factories.

Then there are the millions of people who don't get paid a dime for working countless hours caring for children, parents, and other family members. They often don't even think of themselves as exploited workers, but their labor saves capitalism untold amounts of money in feeding, clothing, and educating its workforce. The United Nations estimates that across the world if unpaid domestic work—two-thirds of which is done by women—were paid at market rates, it would be worth $16 trillion, which is 70 percent of the world's total economic output.[4]

---

4. I'm trying to avoid giving citations, but I have to for this one because it's so staggering: "Unpaid Work and Policy-Making: Towards a Broader Perspective of Work and Employment." It's a United Nations report from 1999, which actually means the numbers would be even higher today because of inflation.

All told, workers make up the majority of people, which is a potential problem for bosses who depend on their labor to keep generating profits. In the early 1800s the poet Percy Shelley wrote these inspiring lines:

Rise, like lions after slumber
In unvanquishable number!
Shake your chains to earth like dew
Which in sleep had fallen on you:
Ye are many—they are few!

Today *ye* are many more than *ye* were in Shelley's day, while *they* are still pretty few. In order to avoid getting overthrown by a mob of unvanquishable lions, much less keep us at our jobs every day making their profits, capitalists need ways to keep us in our place. This is where oppression comes in. Oppression refers to the systemic mistreatment of some group of people on the basis of their ethnicity, gender, disability, sexual identity, or some other factor. It both weakens specific groups of people and keeps them divided from others with whom they could potentially unite.

Note the word systemic—as in something rooted in societal institutions, not unpleasant individual interactions. Men are not oppressed by women, no matter how many angst-ridden songs they write about having their hearts broken. Sexism, racism, and other oppressions are often thought of as individual prejudices—stupid or mean ideas passed down from one generation to the next. This often shifts the focus onto ordinary people—especially poor and working-class ones who aren't trained to subtly disguise their prejudice the way some with better educations are. But oppression comes straight from the top of society. It's about some people getting worse educations, job and housing opportunities, and health care than others, and being made to feel through advertising, schools, and interactions with police and other authorities that they are second-class citizens.

Exploitation and oppression are partners. It's impossible to imagine the exploitation of African Americans through slavery and sharecropping without the racism that held them to be subhuman, just as there is no way that women could be paid less than their male counterparts without a sexist framework that they should be expected to prioritize family over work. More indirectly, the oppression of people with disabilities allows employers to not spend some of their profits on creating workplaces that are widely accessible.

One group whose oppression is often not talked about is the working class—including its straight white men. Workers go to inferior schools, receive substandard health care, and are often treated with contempt by societal institutions. When workers protest or strike, they can be handled roughly by the police and courts in ways that would never fly for those in the middle or upper classes. But the core of workers' oppression takes place, unsurprisingly, at work, where laws meant to be universal simply don't apply. There is no freedom of speech or assembly on company time, and a business's legally binding contracts—like pension agreements—with its workers are somehow less legally binding than its contracts—like loans—with bank executives.

But oppression is also an entirely separate thing from exploitation, with very different characteristics. Not only that, but each form of oppression has its own unique features and history that have to be understood on their own. The oppression of women, as we have seen, has existed for thousands of years, while the oppression of ethnic groups like the Italians and Irish in the United States only lasted a couple of generations. Exploitation remains a constant fact of life, but oppressions can rise and fall in intensity. Homophobia is still a major problem, but it has been wonderfully weakened in recent decades, thanks to the movement for LGBT equality. The oppression of Muslims, on the other hand, has grown horribly worse in the age of the "war on terror." The fact that each oppression is unique is the reason that it is such an effective tool for dividing people against each other and getting them to buy into other people's oppressions even as they suffer their own. It's also true, however, that people's shared experience of some sort of oppression can be a powerful basis for coming together. But that's a subject for the next section. We're still in the gloomy part of the book.

The point here is that the much-hyped freedoms of capitalism are mostly limited to a tiny minority that has the resources to make truly free choices. Emperors and slave-owners from centuries past would not be totally unfamiliar with this variety of freedom.

Anarchy: Competition and Crisis

Yet even the richest straight white men are not immune to capitalism's destructive ways. After all, they do live on this planet, and unless our wildest paranoid suspicions that they are secretly building a moon colony for themselves turn out to be true, they and their children are going to face the consequences of climate change just like the rest of us. Rich people with multiple homes can of course ride out natural disasters a lot more easily than poor people with nowhere to go, but as Hurricane Sandy showed when it submerged the actual Wall Street, there really is nowhere to hide from a planetary problem. But despite the hopes of many environmentalists, capitalism is doing almost nothing to address global warming even as it has started to hit close to the most expensive homes.

Emphasis on the word *doing*. There's plenty of talk about stopping climate change coming from corporate and government leaders. Every

ere are high-profile conferences where brilliant scientists are into desperately plead for a change in energy policy while business
and government leaders politely listen and then do nothing. They
know what the scientists are saying is true, but they are incapable of
thinking outside the logic of capitalism. This was best captured by a
New York Times article following the announcement that the United
States would soon surpass Saudi Arabia as the world's leading oil producer, which was described as "good news for the United States," but
"more sobering for the planet"—as if both could be true at the same
time. This is the most extreme possible version of "American excep-
tionalism" imaginable—as if the United States could build a border
fence high enough to block out rising levels of carbon dioxide.

The people running this country aren't idiots, with some obvious exceptions. The problem is that as powerful as they are compared with us, they are not the true masters of society. Capitalism is
run not by capitalists but by capital itself. Marx quotes an English
union leader about how this relationship works:

> Capital eschews no profit, or very small profit, just as Nature was
> formerly said to abhor a vacuum. With adequate profit, capital is
> very bold. A certain 10 percent will ensure its employment any-
> where; 20 percent certain will produce eagerness; 50 percent, pos-
> itive audacity; 100 percent will make it ready to trample on all
> human laws; 300 percent, and there is not a crime at which it
> will scruple, nor a risk it will not run, even to the chance of its
> owner being hanged.

If it seems I'm making capital sound like some mysterious evil
force that gets inside people's heads like Sauron in *Lord of the Rings*,
that's because I am.[5] Only I prefer an image from *The Fifth Element*,

5. Let Adam Smith have his free market and invisible hand. I'll take the descrip-
tion of bosses clutching profit reports and hissing, "yessss, my precious."

a movie in which you can tell someone has been taken over by "The Great Evil" when a dark ooze (which happens to look like crude oil) starts to run down his forehead. A bit over the top? Possibly, but when I think about oil company executives pressuring governments to let them build more pipelines and sink more wells, even as they know that they might be sealing the planet's fate, I can't help but imagine black liquid slowly trickling down from their hundred-dollar haircuts.

When the ooze of capital enters a capitalist's brain, the main emotion that it manipulates is not greed—although there's plenty of that too—but fear. Capitalists are driven by the fear that if they don't increase profits, someone else will who could eventually put them out of business. Here is the second great flaw of Adam Smith's understanding of capitalism. Blind competition between capitalists really does produce an Invisible Hand of sorts, but this hand can destroy just as easily as it can create. A society that rewards selfishness and punishes sharing does not work very well even for some of those at the top of the capitalist food chain—and it's a disaster for the rest of us. Far from being a reflection of human nature, pure individualism is violently alien to the human experience. We have always depended upon one another, as well as other species, for survival and happiness.

The failure of blind competition is just as evident economically as it is ecologically. Capitalists don't automatically profit from exploiting their workers. The product has to be sold in order to make a return on their investment, which means it's important to not produce too much. But overproduction is just what inevitably occurs in any profitable industry, not because individual capitalists can't control themselves but because they can't control their competition. If one company is making a killing on smartphones, other companies will jump in the market, and then others, until there are many more smartphones being made than people willing and able to buy them. The problem is exacerbated by the drive to pay workers as little as possible, which leads to most consumers not having enough money to buy all the extra crap created by capitalism. The system tries to get around this problem for a time by allowing people and businesses to go into debt to keep buying products with money that they don't really have. Eventually, however, the bills come due, consumers stop buying, companies start laying off workers who themselves stop buying, and the economy goes into a downward spiral known as a recession.

Engels wrote that capitalism combines the tyranny of each boss over his workers with the anarchy of all the bosses' blind competition with one another on the market. This has been a regular feature of capitalism since its inception. Economics textbooks feature lots of charts showing a perfect harmony of supply and demand, but the real thing has instead been a wild ride of booms and recessions that even the most powerful industrialists have been unable to predict, much less control—although most of them are able to get through the stormy times okay by tossing some of us overboard.

Every recession brings about the ironic combination of empty foreclosed houses and abandoned shuttered factories with increased rates of homelessness and unemployment. Many of us have become so accustomed to capital's way of seeing the world that this doesn't strike us as immoral and illogical. Capitalism imposes the alien values of capital on human beings. Education is transformed from the ability to think for ourselves about the world around us into test results measuring the basic literacy and ability to sit still necessary to be good future employees. Neighborhoods are no longer communities who look after one another but blocks of property values that are meant to relentlessly rise even if that gentrification will force many of the people we've known for years to have to leave.

In recent years, the Supreme Court has helpfully spelled out for anyone who didn't already know it that human beings are second-class citizens in a world run by capital. Its *Citizens United v. FEC* ruling infamously declared that "corporations are people," and therefore have a constitutionally protected right to free speech, which for a corporation means throwing tons of money at politicians. At the same time, the court has been regularly restricting the rights of actual people to protest in many locations or be protected from being detained by police and spied on by the government for virtually any reason. It raises the question of whether the court will soon add a corollary to *Citizens United*: "corporations are people, but people aren't people." It isn't just in the United States that capital outranks humans. Capital is a global citizen, able to move freely across borders, even as country after country builds walls and cracks down on people who try to do the same.

What Adam Smith brilliantly understood was that capitalism created a world of freedom. The part he got wrong was that the citizens of this world would not be people but capital, a parasite that uses humanity as a host body to multiply itself even as it weakens our own natural instincts for love, compassion, and possibly even self-preservation.

5.

Who's in Charge?

As children, we are told a story: Once upon a time there was a dashing economic system named Capitalism, and it was the fairest economic system of them all. One day, Capitalism met Democracy, the fairest political system of them all, and together they lived happily ever after.

Life has a way of making us skeptical of fairy tales, but we still believe this one, despite all the evidence that capitalism is far from monogamous. All types of political systems have shacked up with capitalism, from parliamentary democracies to military dictatorships to whatever that thing is in Washington, DC, where the people with bad tans and fake hair yell at each other for the cameras. The world's first democracy in ancient Greece didn't know about capitalism, while the Nazi regime of Adolf Hitler helped some corporations make terrific profits.[1]

---

1. Such as Ford, General Motors, and IBM. The official name of the Nazis, by the way, was the National Socialist Party. This is the most horrifying distortion of the socialist label but far from the only one, as we'll see in chapter 9.

The main point of the equation *capitalism* = *democracy* is not to accurately understand either concept but to establish the inverse: *socialism* = *tyranny.* These formulas were proven correct in many minds in 1989, when the peoples of Eastern Europe overthrew their supposedly "communist" regimes as they protested their lack of democratic rights and their isolation from the global capitalist economy.

Two decades later, however, another revolutionary year challenged the old math. Whereas in 1989 there were democratic revolutions against regimes that called themselves communist, 2011 saw the fight for democracy break out across the capitalist world. It began with the "Arab Spring" revolutions in Tunisia and Egypt, continued with the occupation of the state capitol in Wisconsin and the massive public square assemblies in Greece and Spain, and ended with the Occupy movement in New York, which itself then spread to cities around the globe. The specifics differed in each country, but everywhere in 2011 movements against inequality and budget cuts quickly turned into generation-defining declarations that a better political system is possible. Protesters created popular assemblies and experienced a form of democracy in which the voices and votes of the rich and powerful don't carry any further than those of anyone else. When Tunisians and Egyptians kicked off the protests against their dictators at the beginning of the year, Western media commentators said that the Arab world was having its "democracy moment." As the protests spread to the elected governments of Europe and North America, it became clear that even countries with elected governments are still waiting for their democracy moment.

You Can't Have Billionaires and Democracy

Full democracy is impossible under an economic system that depends on our lack of freedom. As the last chapter described, capitalism allows us to choose what to buy and sell in the marketplace, but it also depends upon a few people owning most of the capital so that the rest of us have no choice over whether or not we want to sell our labor. A system like this simply cannot allow the majority of people to vote on whether or not this setup should be changed. Instead, capitalist democracies grant us the right to vote, but about what, exactly?

Can we democratically decide whether a company should lay off its workers? No. Do we have a say over whether that company can at least not give its executives bonuses while laying off workers? No. Okay, fine. That's private enterprise. Can we vote on whether our government will spy on us? No.

In 2013 Edward Snowden blew the whistle on the vast domestic surveillance system of the National Security Agency (NSA). "You can't have 100 percent security and also then have 100 percent privacy and zero inconvenience," lectured Barack Obama. "We're going have to make some choices as a society." Who did Obama mean by "we"? Would there be a series of public forums in every community debating the NSA's powers or private negotiations between the military-industrial complex and tech company executives? The answer to that question tells us who makes the real decisions under capitalism.

Of course, many of us aren't even allowed to vote. You might not think this has been a major problem since the franchise was extended to women in the Nineteenth Amendment and guaranteed for African Americans with the Voting Rights Act.[2] In fact, the number of Americans barred from voting because they are not citizens or be-

---

2. Actually the Voting Rights Act (VRA) was greatly weakened by the Supreme Court in 2013's *Shelby County v. Holder* on the grounds of the following dubious logic: The VRA is no longer necessary because Black people are no longer prevented from voting thanks to the VRA. I'm really glad the Supreme Court isn't my father's doctor: *Well, Mr. Katch, now that your heart is beating regularly, let's get that pacemaker out of there.*

cause they are currently or formerly incarcerated is almost 10 percent of the voting-age population. That's more than the margin of victory in most presidential elections.

Then there are cities where the entire population has been stripped of its right to vote for the people in charge. The most well known is Detroit, which in the face of bankruptcy was put under the direct control of an unelected financial manager. Everybody knows that Detroit is broke because the auto companies abandoned it, but those company executives get to enjoy their democratic rights in their new hometowns while the unemployed former workers they left behind bear the political punishment.

Finally, even on the issues that are put up to democratic vote, we are saddled with a two-party system in which the "liberal" Democratic Party might be one of the most criminal organizations in modern history. If you think I'm exaggerating, consider that it's the Democrats who:

- fought the Civil War on the side of slavery
- created Jim Crow segregation after they lost that war
- dropped the only nuclear weapons on a civilian population in history
- stole a third of Mexico's land and forced the Cherokee and other tribes on the infamous "trail of tears"
- killed millions in the wars in Korea and Southeast Asia
- doubled the country's prison population under Bill Clinton
- deported over two million immigrants under Barack . . . you get the picture.

The point is not that there is anything better about Republicans, many of whom probably look at the list above and sigh with envy, but that both major US parties are completely devoted to the priorities of the tiny class that runs this country. Each party may be paid to look out for a particular industry (Republicans get lots of oil money while Democrats are preferred by the tech industry), but sometimes they propose different strategies to achieve the same end, such as whether the United States should destroy Middle Eastern countries with or without the approval of the United Nations.

More often, their differences are even less substantial and are almost entirely about how to get different voting blocs to support the same policies. Republicans proudly announce budget cuts by declaring that they are weaning us off our pathetic addiction to public services like schools and hospitals. Democrats blame Republicans for making them pass budget cuts even when the Democrats are in the majority, and then when they lose that majority they promise to fight like hell against those evil Republican budget cuts. Essentially, the Democrats are the loud guy in the bar pretending to be held back by his friends to keep him from going after someone he has absolutely no intention of fighting.

People who are frustrated with the two-party system frequently talk about the government being broken. But the government works just fine for the One Percent—those corporate tax breaks and bank bailouts get passed right on time. And even when Congress is unable to pass any legislation, the government manages to bomb rural villages, deport parents and separate them from their children, and approve new locations for oil drilling just the same. The only broken part of the government is that small part over which we are allowed to have any say.

It is impossible to have a society with vast economic inequality that does not also have vast political inequality. Here's another way to put it: you can have billionaires or you can have democracy, but you cannot have a lot of both.

To understand why, we first have to wrap our heads around just how much a billion dollars is, because unless you are a billionaire—and that is not the target demographic of this book—I guarantee you don't get it. We tend to use the word *billion* to refer to some countless number just shy of infinity, a ludicrous exaggeration of a million not much different than fake numbers like *bajillion* and *shlazillion*.[3] A billion is an actual number; a thousand millions, to be precise. But it is a ludicrous amount of money for one person to own.

The typical family in the United States (forget most of the world) has about $75,000 in net worth. A billion dollars is 13,000 times more than that. If that typical all-American family were to stack its wealth in 75,000 individual dollar bills lined end to end, it would extend 7.2 miles. "Son, that's taller than Mount Everest," Dad might proudly say as he takes a satisfied puff on his pipe and Sparky gives a bark of approval.[4] But if billionaire and ex–New York City mayor Michael Bloomberg showed up and did the same thing, his $25 billion in wealth would stretch all the way to the moon . . . and back . . . five times.

Back on Earth, vast discrepancies in wealth lead to vast discrepancies in power—over all of us. Most readers of this book could probably use an extra thirteen thousand dollars, to pay off their student loans, put something away for retirement, or finally get a car that they can count on. Imagine what unpleasant, embarrassing, or even immoral tasks you might agree to do in exchange

---

3. Nobody actually says *shlazillion*, but I'm trying to make that a thing—as in "There were a shlazillion people at that protest!" or "*Socialism . . . Seriously* is selling shlazzy copies, yo." Help me out: #shlazillion

4. In my imaginary family there is no dog, just a fourteen-year-old boy named Sparky who is going through a strange phase. Sorry if that wasn't clear.

for thirteen thousand dollars. . . . Okay, stop imagining. That was disgusting.

Here's my point: since a billion dollars is thirteen thousand times what the average American owns, a billionaire could give you thirteen thousand dollars to do that undesirable thing and it would cost him the equivalent of one dollar. By the same scale, for a hundred dollars, a billionaire can spend $1.3 million in regular people money, which can buy the support of both candidates in most Congressional races, or pay the salaries of a dozen people to promote his agenda in a think tank or bogus grassroots organization. Having a billion dollars endows him with Godlike powers, and the number of billionaires in the United States has risen from thirteen in 1982 to more than four hundred today. We are seeing the rise of a new race of supermen, and they're not the good guys.

This isn't about petty jealousy. That money came from us! The growing wealth of the superrich coincides with declining wealth for the rest of us—not just our personal savings, but the collective wealth of our schools and post offices, our job security and health benefits, and expectations that our kids will have it better than we do. Economic inequality inevitably leads to political inequality, and just as the rich have been gaining political power, we have been losing it. We aren't just poorer; we're weaker and less organized. We work longer hours, pay more for health care, scramble to deal with more precarious childcare arrangements. We face more repression from law enforcement when we try to protest—or, if we are immigrants, Muslims, or African Americans, even when we don't.

Democracy is measured not just by political structures but by the political strength of the people. In Hal Draper's fascinating series of books about Karl Marx, he notes that in Marx's time the word *democracy* was just coming into popular use and that it had multiple meanings.[5] In addition to referring to a political system based on elections and individual liberties, democracy could also mean the popular will and mass movements. The Chartist movement in England, which fought for voting rights to be extended to the working class, referred to itself as *the democracy*. There is an echo of this older usage today in the popular protest chant: *This is what democracy looks like!* For the most part, however, our definition—and understanding—of democracy has become unfortunately limited to a set of laws. Socialists retain the older, more multifaceted definition because it makes it clear that democracy is something that has to be constantly fought for, even when we live in a political system that calls itself democracy.

Get to Know "Your" Government

Every state hides its unaccountable authority over us by claiming to be so connected to us that accountability is unnecessary. There is supposed to be no difference between us and our government. The US government refers to itself in court cases as "The People" just as Stalinist dictatorships call themselves "People's Republics." This isn't a new development. Frederick the Great of Prussia justified his monarchy by claiming that "the prince is to the nation he governs what the head is to the man; it is his duty to see, think, and act for the whole community."

In truth the first role of states has always been to see, think, and act for the ruling classes of their time, be they slave owners, feudal aristocrats, or transnational corporations. Marx and Engels wrote in *The Communist Manifesto* that the role of capitalist states was to be "a committee for managing the common affairs of the whole bour-

---

5. It's a four-volume series called *Karl Marx's Theory of Revolution*.

geoisie." This is a vital function because capitalists are too blinded by competition in pursuit of immediate profits to engage in long-term planning. Capitalists are like children, and it's the state's job to be the grownup pushing the shopping cart while capitalists sit in the front and make a grab for whatever they want, leaving the state to clean up their spills and put the five boxes of Frosted Flakes back on the shelf.

Capitalists need the state not just to babysit them but to create the basic conditions that make profitable investment possible. The developing capitalist world observed by Adam Smith only existed because of British "enclosure" laws that outlawed the long tradition of common land, which forced millions of poor people to leave the countryside and sell their labor in towns and cities. In the United States, capitalism was greatly helped by some of the Supreme Court's earliest rulings that business contracts and private property were more important than democracy. In the case of *Fletcher v. Peck*, for example, the court ruled that the Georgia legislature could not overturn a land deal that had been passed by previous lawmakers—even though it turned out almost all of them had been bribed to pass the deal! This principle that punishing business crimes is less important than creating a stable investment climate has been the law—or lack of law—of the land ever since.

One of the never-ending debates in American politics is about something known as "the role of government." Conservatives are usually the ones arguing for "small government," and yet they are huge fans of the vast armed wings of the state that make up by far the biggest aspect of government bureaucracy: the military, police, border patrol, and spy agencies. These are the state's core functions, the repressive apparatus at the heart of every society where some have and others don't. *New York Times* columnist Thomas Friedman once wrote approvingly that "McDonald's cannot flourish without

McDonnell Douglas, the designer of the U.S. Air Force F-15. And
the hidden fist that keeps the world safe for Silicon Valley's tech-
nologies to flourish is called the U.S. Army, Air Force, Navy and
Marine Corps." Similarly, the finance whiz kids in your local city
cannot thrive in their gleaming new waterfront luxury apartments
without the peace of mind of knowing that the police are all over
the far larger numbers of poor kids in the surrounding neighborhoods. What conservatives find to be "government tyranny" are
those additional services taken on by twentieth-century governments
around the world in response to popular demand: caring for the elderly and the sick, monitoring discrimination and the food supply,
and so on.

Liberals (some of them at least) rightly reject the cruel conservative view that the only functions of the state should be repression and
corporate catering, and instead assert that government can play a positive role in promoting human welfare. Liberals hold up the decades
after World War II as a model, when rich people and corporations
paid much higher taxes, unions were at their peak, and a social safety
net was created through programs for the poor, sick, unemployed,
and elderly. All of this is correct, but let's think twice about proclaiming the postwar era as a golden age to be re-created. This was a period
in which the US policy was to create whites-only suburbs and Black
urban ghettos,[6] persecute hundreds of thousands of communists,
bring the world to the edge of nuclear war, and destroy Korea, Vietnam, Guatemala, and Iran through wars and coups. Then there's the
fact that the United States was enjoying the greatest economic boom
in world history—which made it possible for rich people to be more
generous without seeing their own wealth decline—only due to the
unique circumstance that every other industrial country had just been

6. Look up "redlining."

bombed to smithereens. That's not something we should count or hope for—recurring.

The point is that even in the golden age of American liberalism, the government was not an agent of the people. It certainly is not now, when it imprisons more of its people than any nation in the world and is constructing enormous cloud facilities with the capacity to monitor all of its people's phone and Internet conversations. The only reason we even know about this world-historic surveillance system is because of the bravery of Edward Snowden, who has been charged with violating the Espionage Act. Espionage, notes journalist Glenn Greenwald, is generally defined as passing secrets to the government's enemies. However, Snowden didn't reveal the NSA's secrets to Iran or China but to the general public. What does that say about how the US government regards its people?

And yet none of the endless debates between Republicans and Democrats about the size of government take up the growing power of what is often referred to in other countries as the "deep state." Understanding the state in this way does not mean we have to fall down the rabbit hole of conspiracy theories, which imagine that everyone in the government is either involved in secret plots or part of the cover-up. There are plenty of real conspiracies that have been uncovered by excellent journalism—the CIA really did introduce crack into Black neighborhoods in Los Angeles, for example, and the journalist who helped to expose that story was basically driven out of mainstream journalism.[7] But for the most part, conspiracy theorists are so intent on searching the deepest corners of the Internet for hidden plots that they don't see that the most obvious conspiracies—like world financial summits and voter suppression—take place right out in the open.

7. The reporter's name was Gary Webb. There's a movie about him called *Kill the Messenger*.

The other problem with most conspiracy theories is that they give the people at the top way too much credit for actually knowing what the hell they're doing. Even the US government, powerful and destructive as it is, is a servant of the dark ooze of capital, which has no master plan other than making more of itself. The Defense Department, for example, is well aware that global warming is the biggest threat out there. It has funded extensive studies and military scenarios preparing for food riots and refugee rampages. But it doesn't occur to the most powerful military force in world history that there is something it can do to thwart the threat of climate change itself. Generals could be planning the invasion of the boardrooms of oil companies to order them to switch energy production to solar and wind. Instead they are waging and planning wars to keep the oil flowing and the temperature rising. No matter how many brilliant scientists and strategists it employs, the Pentagon maintains the mindset of a street cop—concerned only about keeping order for the bosses.

Just as capitalism combines the tyranny of the individual owner with the anarchy of all the bosses' competition with each other, it combines the repression of each state over its own population with the chaos of every state's competition with every other for control of global trade and military dominance. For all of the growing central and secret powers accruing inside the government, we don't even get the benefit of that power being used for rational purposes. Socialists call this global anarchy *imperialism*, and it includes everything from warfare to diplomacy to trade agreements, whatever can give one nation a leg up in what the English used to call the Great Game.[8] Part of the game today

---

8. Specifically "the Great Game" referred to the nineteenth-century British rivalry with Russia for control of Central Asia. This smug name for a century of wars and horrors is a great illustration of the English penchants for understatement, dry wit, and genocide.

involves attending global summits about global threats like climate change and nuclear arms, not to genuinely collaborate on solutions but to try to make it look like it's your rivals' fault that you didn't.

Conspiracy theories sound radical, but they actually provide a false comfort for those who are overwhelmed by the complexities of the world's problems and would prefer to understand them as a plot carried out by a few all-powerful actors. Some people find it easier to view the September 11 attacks as a "false flag" operation carried out within the deepest corners of the Pentagon than to deal with it as one of the many unpredictable but inevitable consequences of the United States waging war across the planet. The truth, which might be more terrifying than a secret all-powerful ruling cabal, is that nobody is fully in charge.

Capitalism puts so much power and wealth in a few hands that from our point of view down below those hands seem to wield complete control. The good news—and the bad news—is that the people in charge of shaping the world for our children often have no clear plan beyond the next election or quarterly earnings report. They veer from crisis to crisis, from the disastrous invasions of Iraq and Afghanistan to the global financial meltdown caused by crooked banks to the ongoing catastrophe of climate change. Ultimately, capitalists find solutions to their crises at our expense—send more troops, close more hospitals—unless our forces are strong enough to stop them.

Most of the time we aren't strong enough, the troops get deployed, the hospitals closed, and cynics conclude that the whole crisis was just a ruse, which only reinforces our sense of powerlessness. But the crises are real, and they can prove to be capitalism's undoing—if there is a viable alternative waiting to replace it.

Damn, that would have been a great cliffhanger if the title of the book hadn't spoiled it.

Part 3:

Socialism

6.

Imagine

"Okay, shut up," you hoarsely whisper. "I'm awake." The voice recognition system in your bed long ago learned to recognize your grouchy Early Day tone and shuts off the alarm. It's 4:30am on the first Tuesday of the month, your day to help open the restaurant.

The only thing worse than working Early Day is working Early Day on a Tuesday, the beginning of the work week. It's nice that we've gotten rid of so many of the old pointless jobs of capitalism (public relations, investment banking, mall security, and so on) and distributed the work that actually needs to get done so that most people just work Tuesdays through Thursdays. But you're not exactly in a grateful mood this early on a cold-ass February morning.

Out of the warm bed you go, stretching quietly to not wake up the person still sleeping. (You can surely do a better job than me imagining the details about who's in your bed.) You stumble down the hall to the bathroom, still feeling your way around this funky old Victorian house. It's a three-monther that you signed up for with some new friends from the restaurant. You barely knew them before moving in, but it's going pretty well.

Many people choose to live in one permanent place the old-fashioned way—especially older generations and those who experienced the trauma of homelessness, which is now considered a bygone horror like smallpox or bubonic plague. One of the first postrevolution priorities for city and neighborhood assemblies was to create well-built and pleasant housing for all who needed it out of the millions of houses, mansions, and offices that capitalism had abandoned, underused, or stupidly used (public relations, investment banking) . . .

But in recent years there has been a growing desire to break out of the "suffocating prison of sameness," as one radical pamphlet called it. The movement for varied housing started out in fevered debates in public squares in Mexico City and Seoul. Although their initial proposals to city assemblies failed to win majorities, their "Mix It Up!" Internet channel became wildly popular among many who had grown up post-capitalism. Within a few months, teenager committees were voting overwhelmingly (and, truth be told, a little bit sneeringly) to demand that varied housing be made available. As has often been the case under socialism, the teens got what they wanted and they turned out to be mostly right.

People of all ages have been signing up to live in what capitalist societies would have called timeshares. The resulting shift of housing stock from perm to temp has of course created a lot more administrative, construction, and design work for the housing sector. But many "Mix It Up!" activists understood this would be the case and signed up for jobs in housing to meet the need that they had created.

You've never worked in housing, which is surprising because sometimes it seems like you've worked every possible job. You aren't even thirty years old and already you've been a kindergarten teacher, an urban forest ranger, a firefighter apprentice, and, most recently, a worker at the plant that retrofits appliances and automobiles that were made under capitalism and therefore designed to consume as much energy as possible and then break down within ten years. You loved the mental challenge of that job, figuring out how to salvage something socially useful from those old pieces of profit-maximizing crap. In a factory job under capitalism you never would have been able to use your brain in that way, much less been allowed to use some of the extra junk to make those hilarious "Hummer-monsters" that still stand outside the bathrooms. Still, after two years among the toxic chemicals and planet-hating plastic of capitalist consumer goods, you were ready for a change.

A few of your friends are "lifers," but you don't understand why anyone would tie themselves to one job for ten or twenty years. Many young people feel the same way, which isn't great for sectors like engineering and research that require long-term expertise and time commitments. The issue is constantly being debated in the elected assemblies, Internet channels, and public squares.

Like most people, you've gone to school during and between most of these jobs, taking and teaching classes in biology, basketball, and erotic communication. You even found yourself, much to your surprise, elected a neighborhood spokesperson during the statewide referendum on whether everyone really needs to know algebra. It's ironic how much your life superficially resembles that of many young people in the last decades of capitalism: bouncing around between temporary jobs while also squeezing in time to take classes. It just goes to show that what matters is often not what you do but whether you are doing it by choice. Okay, that's enough philosophizing in the shower. Time to go to work.

It's a typical February morning in Philadelphia, which is to say typical for the year 2050 when there is no such thing as typical weather. Because socialism didn't come soon enough to stop global temperatures from rising three degrees past the climate change tipping point, weather patterns are far less predictable. Yesterday it was 65 degrees. Today it's in the low 30s. At least oil, coal, and gas have been completely phased out and . . . wait, did you say the year 2050? You keep doing that. It's crazy that it's already 2051.

A couple blocks from home you hop on an express tram zipping toward Center City. The atmosphere is perversely fun as the riders and driver loudly grumble about how much they hate Early Day and argue whether it's worse than Late Day. As you approach downtown on Kelly Drive the mood lifts as you all watch the sun rising over the Schuylkill River.

It takes about the same time to reach downtown as it would have in a personal car forty years ago. The extra time it takes to pick up passengers along the way is mitigated by the time saved from having barely any traffic and fewer stoplights. Most city roads became private-car free ten years ago so the only vehicles on Kelly Drive are trams, delivery and utility trucks, and the occasional ambulance. One of the unanticipated benefits was the windfall of space where all the parked cars used to be. Block committees gleefully tore up the asphalt and built gardens, sculptures, and in one hipster area (which somehow still exists), rows of shuffleboard tables. Your block created an herb garden, and you often return there to pick rosemary and cilantro.

(The debate over banning cars, by the way, lasted for years after tram lines were laid across the city—at times it was quite bitter. Car lovers were a minority, but a passionate one. They were not persuaded by the argument that they could still go out for drives on highways and were only appeased—mostly—when the city assembly agreed to convert some of the old roads in Fairmount Park into a driving course.)

You get to work just in time to help open up. After setting up the kitchen you grab some coffee and a muffin and sit down at a small table against the wall. Some mornings you like to join the social diners at one of the long tables, but you're a little preoccupied today so you finish breakfast quickly and get back to the kitchen. Work is busy, not because there are more diners than usual but because a bunch of them want to be served in the old-fashioned style at their tables rather than just getting food from the kitchen themselves. You don't mind—it's fun actually—but it means you've got to hustle, especially when the three classes of eight-year-olds come in at eleven to learn how to make oatmeal cookies.

That was your favorite part of grade school—the weekly trips to different workplaces. You were the first third grader to figure out how to splice a fiber-optic cable, and the slowest at climbing up and down the manhole ladders. It still blows your mind that before socialism people under a certain age had to sit in school all day without ever seeing work, and people above that age had to do the opposite.

The day goes by quickly and happily, until you screw up just as you're getting ready to leave after the lunch rush. Once again, you forgot to charge someone for her meal. Each year the whole money thing feels increasingly pointless in a society in which everyone has more than enough of what they need and plenty of what they want. But money is still the main way for planning committees to keep track of how goods and services are being distributed and used. Thanks in part to your forgetfulness, the restaurant had only a vague estimate of how much food it served in January, which pissed off some assemblies and committees because there's a friendly competition going on with New York City to reduce unnecessary transportation costs and energy consumption from excess food shipments. Okay, it's not so friendly. Even under socialism, Philadelphia hates New York.

After your sheepish exit from work, you hop on a public bike to go see your uncle. This visit has been putting you on edge all day. Uncle Mike is a die-hard "profitist." He was a rising young executive for a big pharmaceutical company before the revolution who found it impossible to reconcile himself to the radical democracy of mass assemblies that replaced the Wall Street/Pentagon regime. He worked alongside other profitists to sabotage the new system, organizing medicine shortages in city hospitals. People died because of Uncle Mike and he was sentenced to ten years in one of Pennsylvania's prisons. (A common joke in those early years was that socialism had gentrified the jails because they had become so much richer and whiter.) He was released a few years early along with most of the other inmates after their networks were broken up and they no longer represented a threat to anyone's safety. He still runs a crank profitist website and gets together with old friends in a coffee shop—which they proudly insist on still calling "Dunkin' Donuts"—to mutter about how much better things used to be.

Your visit with Uncle Mike is short and uncomfortable. You don't wish him more suffering than he's already had, but you also don't like him and don't fully understand why you are supposed to see him. This question offends your mother. He is your family:

no other explanation is necessary. But many people your age have a much wider definition of family that can include close friends, favorite teachers, and kids that they have grown close to in their shifts at the 24-hour child care centers. Why should you have a special obligation to someone you detest just because he is your mom's brother? So you and your mother argue.

On your way home from your uncle's, you wonder if there are more arguments under socialism. It can be tedious for every major decision to be democratically decided, especially when there are no easy answers. The question about keeping stores open twenty-four hours, for example, which pits a minor convenience for many consumers against a more substantial sacrifice for a small number of workers,, has been reversed multiple times over the years. It can be exhausting to constantly question old assumptions and habits, and to not have the false reassurance that everything will be okay because the people in charge are wiser than you. You imagine that socialism is a bit like parenthood: a new world of responsibilities that are sometimes overwhelming but also impossible to imagine not having. (Of course you're not even thinking about how overwhelming child-rearing was before socialism, when society's most important job was almost entirely put on the shoulders of just one or two parents.)

Older folks can have an especially hard time with the new responsibilities, but even you sometimes tune everything out for a couple of weeks and just go around with your headphones on, like those pictures from the last years of capitalism. Of course, you know that back then people got into lots of arguments too, much worse than the ones today because they weren't aimed at solving anything but just blaming each other for the problems they had no power to fix.

*Maybe you'll drop by a philosophy discussion tonight—
there's a Tuesday one at a bar in your neighborhood—to bounce
some of these ideas around. But first, you think as you pull up in
front of your beautiful Victorian three-monther, it is time for a
well-deserved Early Day nap.*

And . . . scene. There you have it: one fairly crappy socialist day.
I decided to imagine a bad day under socialism for a few reasons.
First, I want to raise our expectations by showing how much better
the world can be even on a relatively bad day. Ice Cube used this
same method in reverse when he rapped, "Nobody I know got killed
in South Central LA. Today was a good day." That gets to my second
reason, which is my dream of becoming known as "The Ice Cube
of communism."[1]

Most importantly, I want to establish from the outset that we're
not talking about a utopia filled with only sunshine and universal
agreement. The first objection that is often raised against socialism
is that it will fall apart at the first sign of disagreement. If I want cars
to be banned and housing to be varied, but you want to go on driving and owning a permanent home, chaos will ensue, followed by
mayhem, culminating in downright pandemonium.

This argument, which at its heart is a claim that ordinary people
aren't capable of democracy in any society, is bunk. It's true that there
might be more daily disagreement—perhaps even a little chaos—in
a society in which so many more people have a say in their life conditions. But this is quite minor compared to the chaos of being over-

---

1. Yeah, I know that these days Ice Cube plays the police in movies instead of
shouting "Fuck them!" with NWA. You're only noticing now that my cultural ref-
erences are embarrassingly outdated?

worked and subject to unjust laws that human beings have grown accustomed to in the name of "order" over a relatively recent period of our species's history.

Let me be clear that this hypothetical day can't tell us anything for certain about socialism—other than the fact that I seem to think it will be written in italics. If we learned anything from my mental exercise, it was the inclinations and limitations of my own imagination. A different writer would have described how socialist Philadelphia would keep warm and well fed without the use of fossil fuels, or what its neighborhoods and architecture would look like once it was freed from the need to boost property values, or where the remnants of racism and sexism still lingered in postrevolutionary society and how they would be addressed.

There are a hundred factors we cannot anticipate that will shape socialism in 2050—sorry, 2051. Where did revolutions break out first and where did they first win? Will the words that are created to describe new forms of strikes and protests come from English or Mandarin, Portuguese or Bengali? How recently has capitalism been overturned in the United States, and how much power do people like Uncle Mike still have? How much of the planet will have become deserts or permanent flood zones? How many resources will new societies have to devote to figuring out ways to adapt eight billion people to a permanently altered climate?

And on happier notes: What gains will the struggles for gender freedom and sexual liberation win before the revolution, and to what degree will the first generation to grow up under socialism have moved beyond rigidly dividing themselves into two genders? How strong will the movements of indigenous and First Nations peoples be, and how will their long-standing anticapitalist worldviews mesh with socialist ideas born in nineteenth-century industrial Europe?

I don't recommend spending too much time daydreaming about these questions and the thousand others like them. Socialism isn't a planned community that can be created in advance but the society that humanity will figure out for itself once it is freed from the profit-centric rules of capitalism. But at a time when socialism has become such a vague ghost, it's not a total waste of time to dream a bit about what concrete forms genuine democracy and equality could take.

People have pursued the dream of a world based on cooperation for thousands of years. Some have given up all their money and joined monasteries to endlessly meditate. Others have spent lots of money and gone to Burning Man to endlessly do drugs. Karl Marx's contribution was the idea that the working class could be the force that could bring this about for everyone, not just for a few people dropping out of society to join a commune.

Workers have this potential because of their numbers and economic power, but more importantly because the only way they can successfully take on their bosses is to organize collectively. It wasn't out of thin air that I came up with those committees and councils in my imaginary socialist day. They have been created in countless workers' revolutions and uprisings over the past century and a half. That's why socialism won't be formed out of the minds of today's socialists but out of the decisions made by tomorrow's workers in the course of their fight for their freedom.

But some imagination is necessary to see how we might get to a hopeful future from a dismal present. Socialists view the world not just as it is but as it can be—for good and for bad. When governments enact laws, we look for how they might abuse their new powers. But when people come together to fight for even the smallest improvement at work, at school, or on the streets, we see the germs of a new form of society.[2]

When protest happens on a larger scale in strike waves and revolutions, socialists are suddenly not the only people who see this potential. But on most days it seems very far away, and socialists are very few in number. In this atmosphere, it might seem corny to imagine a day under socialism—even my own neurotic version where everybody whines and argues despite being surrounded by material abundance and supportive communities.

"Look at the movies that we see all the time," radical philosopher Slavoj Žižek told a crowd at Occupy Wall Street. "It's easy to imagine the end of the world—an asteroid destroying all of life, and so on—but we cannot imagine the end of capitalism." It isn't just the Hollywood dream factory that has lost the capacity to dream. Naomi Klein reports that even most of the climate scientists whose research has proven that our current economic structures are driving most species to extinction are unable to picture those structures being overturned. "Changing the earth's climate in ways that will be chaotic and disastrous is easier to accept," Klein writes, "than the prospect of changing the fundamental, growth-based, profit-seeking logic of capitalism."

Facts and research aren't enough to successfully challenge the only way of life we've ever known. We need imagination to show how different the world can be and we need power to make that world a reality. Socialists are ultimately judged by how well they can get those two wild horses of power and imagination to run in the same direction.

Revolutionaries have long warned about capitalism's civilization-threatening tendencies, most famously when Rosa Luxemburg declared during World War I that society faced the choice between

---

2. We're excitable, if nothing else.

"socialism or barbarism." But socialism is so much more than just avoiding Armageddon. It would be the first time that humanity's potential would not be shackled by a lack of resources or a system that keeps those resources in a few hands. It was in that spirit that Marx wrote that the end of capitalism would mark the closing of the "prehistory of human society." Socialism, in other words, is necessary both to prevent the decline of human civilization and to begin a new one more worthy of the name.

7.

Workers' Power

In October 2013 workers in the Bay Area Rapid Transit (BART) system went on strike, disrupting the daily commute for employees of San Francisco powerhouses like Google and Twitter. Tech company executives who like to think of themselves as rebellious "disruptors" of old economic models were furious that they had been disrupted by what they considered the most outdated relic of them all—a labor union.

"Get 'em back to work, pay them whatever they want, and then figure out how to automate their jobs so this doesn't happen again," fumed Richard White, the CEO of something called UserVoice, whose website boasts that it helps organizations "find a better way to listen to their users' voices."

Richard White certainly wasn't in the mood to listen to the voices of BART workers that morning, because they were reminding him that even Silicon Valley can't run without train operators and bus drivers. Like all capitalists, but perhaps even more so, tech bosses prefer to imagine that society has no classes, only millions of individuals freely buying and selling their goods and labor to one another. If a few of them have more money than they can spend while most of us have more needs than we can afford, the rest of us shouldn't get jealous. Just create the next big app and join them!

For four days in October, the BART strike punctured this fantasy by reminding our Captains of Digital Industry that the working class is real. Even worse (from their point of view), this class isn't just an unfortunate object of pity but a potential powerhouse in its own right whose strength comes from unity, solidarity, and other age-old concepts that Bay Area bosses must have thought had been buried a thousand TED talks ago.

Class Is Always in Session

Until the Occupy movement and its talk about the One Percent, class was practically an invisible topic. Even today, when the word is uttered on television it is usually following "middle." Everyone in the United States is supposedly middle class, whether we make $25,000 a year or $250,000 a year. It would be unpatriotic to let ourselves be divided by that extra zero.

In the national mythology, one small segment of society is The Rich and a slightly larger one is The Poor. The media almost always illustrate this latter group with pictures of African Americans, which sneakily transforms even supposed discussions about class into coded ones about race. By default, everybody else is in the middle, which is useless for understanding class but great for disguising it. If everyone is middle class, then millions of daily episodes of class conflict—between managers and managed, landlords and land-lorded, and so on—become just so many random personality beefs.

If we wanted a more accurate picture of the middle class by dividing the US population into three categories based on income, the middle third would be those who make between $30,000 and $50,000 a year. This at least gives us a better sense of reality than television, where *Two Broke Girls* can apparently afford a swanky Brooklyn apartment with hardwood floors that in the real Brooklyn would be home to "Two Bankers' Kids."

But income alone still doesn't tell us that much about class, and not just because most of rich people's wealth comes not from what they earn but what they own—companies, mansions, stocks, artwork, and probably incredible skin care products extracted from the blood of endangered tigers. Class isn't just about wealth.

Throughout history, classes have been defined more by what they do than by how much they make. Peasants, merchants, landowners, slaves, craftspeople: these categories tell us something about people's wealth, but much more about the role they play in society. This is still the most useful way to understand class, although it's understandable why many tech bosses would rather not. As one memorable tweet during the BART strike put it: "'Can you believe the salary these BART guys get to drive a train?'—someone whose job is making internet ads more clickable."

Classes are categories based on the roles different groups of people play in the ongoing production and reproduction of their society's needs and wants. Capitalist society has three main classes:

- Capitalists, who own what Marx calls "the means of production," meaning the wealth that they use to invest in land and tools in order to create more wealth (that is, profits).
- Workers, whose labor the capitalists have to buy because land and tools can't turn themselves into profits.

- A middle class of managers, professionals, and small business owners, whose work combines aspects of both capitalists and workers.

These classes are not defined by income. When autoworkers unionized in the 1930s, they went from poverty wages to owning motorboats in a matter of two decades, but they were still autoworkers.[1] Today if a fast-food worker goes on strike, he'll find less support from a Starbucks manager making $40,000 than he will from an airline pilot making twice that much, because the pilot has also experienced fighting alongside her coworkers against a company's efforts to squeeze them for more profits. Although it's true that, as we learned in kindergarten, we are all snowflakes with our own unique personalities, it's equally true—and not taught in school—that many of our opinions and basic political instincts are shaped by our class experiences. As a result, each class has its own distinct characteristics.

The point of dividing society into these classes is not to neatly assign everyone to their proper category, which is impossible since class lines blur across boundaries. A handful of pro athletes make more money than many CEOs, but they also remain workers—as they are reminded when they dare to question a coach's decision and the press screams at them to "Shut up and play!" More commonly, nurses and teachers face speedups and harassment like other workers but still retain some of the middle-class status and decision-making

---

1. Sadly, these days new hires in the auto industry are making wages much closer to the miserable pre-union level of pay. But they are still autoworkers, so they have the power to win back their old gains—if they can get the union to fight the way it used to back when it was filled with socialists. That's right, we pretty much built the labor movement—no big deal. Check out Sharon Smith's *Subterranean Fire* for the overall story or Farrell Dobbs's *Teamster Rebellion* if you want to read about one amazing strike.

power that their jobs used to have before health care and public education were corporatized. The most effective nurses' and teachers' unions are the ones whose members fully understand that they are no longer—if they ever were—professionals working in partnership with their hospitals and school boards but skilled workers being exploited by them. These complicated examples show that class cannot be oversimplified, not that class isn't a useful category. In fact, they demonstrate one of the key characteristics of class: conflict with other classes. Each class can only be defined in terms of tension-filled relationships to the others. Without owners, there are no workers. Without workers, no supervisors.

Capitalists make up the most powerful class, of course. They have insider access to all levels of government and can determine the fate of entire towns by opening or closing a factory. Their children are educated at elite institutions that instill in them a supreme confidence that they are qualified to run the world. From the point of view of most of us down below, the capitalist class seems to have complete control. In fact, capitalists are mentally hobbled by the daily cutthroat competition with each other demanded by their profit system, which leads them to make short-term decisions like young children who don't yet understand that if they eat the candy bar now, they won't be able to eat it later: don't pay corporate taxes today even though tomorrow the government won't be able to fix roads and bridges your employees need to get to work; don't lose money from ending oil drilling today even though if you keep going, your grandchildren may think of New York City as that funny place where the buildings stick out of the water. Capitalists veer from crisis to crisis, from the disastrous invasions of Iraq and Afghanistan to the global financial meltdown caused by crooked banks to the ongoing catastrophe of climate change. Of course, one of the benefits of being the most powerful class is that you don't have to be a genius at crisis management as long as you can use your traditional "make everyone else clean it up!" solution—which is why we need a system not ruled by omnipotent five-year-olds.

When people mention the working class these days, they often simply mean people who don't have much money. Socialists don't define workers by what they lack but by the potential power they possess. When workers sell their labor, they are put to work in large complex organizations—factories, hospitals, transportation, and retail networks, and so on—which they operate collectively. This complex division of labor allows relatively small groups of workers to produce or make possible huge productivity and profits—or jeopardize them by going on strike. Those few thousand Bay Area transit workers can cause a much greater economic disruption than a similar number of poor farmers or Walmart managers.

Some complex organizations are harder places for workers to organize themselves. Most unions were born during an era when tens of thousands of workers were concentrated in factory districts in large cities. Today many factories have been moved to isolated rural areas and workers are struggling to figure out how to organize themselves in companies with decentralized structures—from fast-food behemoths with thousands of small franchises to tech giants that rely on temp labor and independent contractors. But figuring it out they are. In recent years, employees have held sit-ins and strikes demanding higher pay and union recognition at McDonald's, Walmart, Uber, and other companies that many thought would be impossible places for workers to organize.

The paradox of working-class power is that it originates in how individual workers are powerless. We sell our labor to a boss because we don't have a choice, not because we enjoy giving up our autonomy for eight to ten hours a day. As sociologist Erik Olin Wright explains, workers only exist as a class because they or their ancestors have been robbed of the land and wealth that would allow them to survive independently. But it is this individual powerlessness that eventually compels workers to come together and organize collectively.[2]

Middle-class people, by contrast, enjoy more individual autonomy than workers, which is why many workers dream of escaping their class and becoming managers or opening up their own businesses. But members of the middle class are pushed around by capitalists just like workers, only without the collective power to resist. The paradox of working-class power applies to the middle class in reverse. The very individualism of the small business owner who "doesn't have to answer to anybody"—which is celebrated as a core American value and envied by many workers—makes the middle class extremely ineffective as a collective body. In times of widespread class struggle, the middle class is like a gang of big toughs squaring off against an army regiment—it's outmatched in terms of both discipline and firepower.

"What is the middle class in the middle of?" asks Michael Zweig in *The Working Class Majority*. "If we answer this question in terms of power instead of income, we see that the middle class is in between the two great social forces in modern society, the working class and the capitalist class." The middle class occupies a murky region where elements of capitalism's two defining classes intermix. "The independent peasant or handicraftsman is cut up into two persons," writes Karl Marx in *Capital*. "As owner of the means of production he is a capitalist; as laborer he is his own wage-laborer." Because the

2. *Eventually* is a convenient word for authors because it can mean strikes will break out next month or next decade. If you're waiting for the class struggle to explode, pack a lunch.

middle class contains traits of both workers and capitalists, it sees it-self as the "everyman" representing all of society—as opposed to the "special interests" of workers (the actual majority of the country) and big capitalists. This is true in the sense that the middle class best rep-resents within itself the class contradictions of capitalism, but that doesn't help it find a way out of those contradictions. Without the individual power of capitalists or the collective power of workers, the political instinct of the middle class is to call on both sides to stop fighting. Because it can't produce an alternative to capitalism that re-ally would give everyone an equal voice, its calls for unity end up being window dressing for the status quo, which makes it an excellent breeding ground for politicians. Most elections feature two candi-dates competing over who can more sincerely pose as an ordinary middle-class guy, as if that is more important than which capitalists are funding their campaign and writing their platform.

The working class, by contrast, has the power to back up its words with action, but it only gains this power through a long process of learning how to organize itself. A hotel cleaner is strug-gling to keep up with the crazy pace of forty room changes a day. She pleads her case to the manager, who tells her if she's not happy she can find another job. A few months later, she comes back to his office, this time with the other fifteen cleaners on her shift. Suddenly the manager is more interested in his workers' unhappiness, partic-ularly because he knows that every minute they stand in his office the hotel is falling further behind the fast pace of room changes that he had been so proud of until this very instant.

The group nature of working-class resistance doesn't just help workers to extract some raises and better conditions from their bosses. It can also, in much more intense moments, point to a pos-sible world without bosses, which makes workers different from many previous exploited classes. When peasants revolted against the big landowner and took over his estate, they usually divided it among themselves into individual plots of land—a fine plan for them that happened to not challenge the larger system of private land ownership. By contrast, if the hotel workers find themselves in a fight in which they have to take over the hotel—perhaps to prevent it from being closed—they wouldn't split the rooms up into a hundred separate new hotels but would instead have to all run the operation together, which would force them to come up with a new collective decision-making structure. Even if these workers are no more interested than peasants in challenging private ownership, the nature of their class pushes them in that direction.

It turns out that there are already hundreds of businesses in the United States that are owned and run by workers. These cooperatives aren't socialist—they exist inside a capitalist economy and have to compete for profit with other companies or else get driven out of business. But they do provide proof of a basic reality that is clear to most workers every time their manager takes a sick day: things run a lot better when there aren't bosses around to bark orders that alternate between being dead wrong and dead obvious. The essence of socialism is that workers can use this collective organization that they have learned under capitalism to create not just cooperative workplaces but a cooperative society geared to meet humanity's needs instead of a competitive one geared to maximize profit.

Poor capitalists. In order to make profits, they must bring workers together and exploit them, but competition with other capitalists forces them to push that exploitation further until the workers resist and create their own organizations whose very existence demonstrates that workers are capable of running the place themselves and calls into question what right capitalists have to own it in the first place. It is this process of inadvertently uniting millions of members of the lower classes into an organized working class that led *The Communist Manifesto* to famously pronounce that what the capitalist class "produces, above all, are its own gravediggers."[3] At the time it was an epic burn, which was one of Marx's specialties. A hundred and fifty years later it can read more like an empty boast.

The working class hasn't managed to bury capitalism yet, but Marx wasn't wrong to say that it could—especially because there were many socialists in his time who actually opposed workers' struggles. These were the utopians who understood the socialist project as one of dreaming up a harmonious society so obviously superior to this nasty one that people of all classes would join together and make the dream a reality. The utopians were mostly middle-class reformers who sympathized with workers' plight under capitalism but viewed strikes as pointless protests that would only push away the factory owners who needed to be convinced to join the socialist cause.

Marx came from a middle-class background himself, yet he viewed class conflict not as a neutral observer but as a participant on the side of the workers. Like the utopians, he recognized that the class struggle produced by capitalism is a nasty business. But unlike the middle-class reformers, he understood that the solution was not to wish the struggle out of existence but for the working class to win it and build a more just society. The great Black abolitionist Frederick Douglass made a similar point about the struggle against slavery:

> If there is no struggle there is no progress. Those who profess to favor freedom and yet deprecate agitation are men who want crops

---

3. Years ago there was a strike of cemetery workers in Queens. I visited the picket line a number of times to show support and I still kick myself for never making a sign about capitalism's gravediggers.

without plowing up the ground; they want rain without thunder and lightning. They want the ocean without the awful roar of its many waters.

This struggle may be a moral one, or it may be a physical one, and it may be both moral and physical, but it must be a struggle. Power concedes nothing without a demand. It never did and it never will.[4]

The simplest definition of Marx's socialism is that it is what society would look like if the working class were in charge. Workers' cooperative organization would extend across industries and society. Equally important, the majority class would be in power for the first time in recorded history, which would lead to the gradual dissolving of classes themselves, since a majority can't live off the exploited labor of a minority. This idea that socialism is defined by the ultimate victory of the working class is Marx's most important contribution, because it took socialism away from fantasies dreamed up in smoke-filled dorm rooms at 3:00 am (or whatever the nineteenth-century version of that was) to an ambitious but sober program rooted in a real social force created by capitalism itself.

Solidarity

Just to be clear, we are talking about potential, not describing reality. Some people think it's enough to discredit socialism by pointing out that most workers today don't agree with it, which is a bit like dis-

---

4. An office I once worked in had a sign that bastardized this great Douglass quote into an employee motivational slogan: *Without struggle, there is no progress.* It makes me wonder if there is some company that specializes in turning icons of the Black freedom struggle into cheesy office directives: *Make sure to file your paperwork—by any means necessary!*

agreeing with great sex on the basis that most people don't have it. But socialists don't claim that a majority of workers are socialists, just that can they become committed to socialist ideas at certain historical moments. (More on this in the next chapter.)

Why should we expect working people to be socialists and believe that their class is capable of running society when they are taught the opposite every day of their lives? From childhoods in underfunded schools to adulthoods in underpaid jobs, working-class people are taught to keep their heads down, follow orders, and keep their bright ideas to themselves. Then we turn on the TV to watch CEOs and action heroes celebrated for being free-spirited, rebellious, and every other quality that's been drummed out of us. This is one of capitalism's nasty habits: degrading people and then blaming them for their degradation. Black men are the last workers hired and the first ones fired, and then are demonized as deadbeat dads who don't provide for their children. Girls are vilified for dressing the very way they've been told to by a thousand magazine covers. Later they will be blamed by those same magazines for neglecting their families to go to work, even while they are being blamed at work for taking time off for their families.

The working class isn't immune to this drumbeat of negativity. Like all human beings, workers are great at thinking bad things about themselves—and even better at thinking them about others. Working people are just as susceptible to racism and sexism as anybody else. Walk outside a corporate office on a summer day while bankers and delivery guys stand together objectifying the passing women, and you'll see that the bonds of class are not necessarily stronger than those of gender. That's why socialists reject the populist approach of dismissing issues like abortion or marriage equality as "distractions" that prevent working people from simply uniting around class issues.[5] First of all, they are class issues—having to take off work to drive to another state for an abortion or being denied a spouse's health insurance plan is a particular hardship for working-class women and LGBT people. Just as importantly, these are issues of freedom and dignity, which matter just as much to people as the size of their paycheck. If some workers ignore—or support—the oppressions of other workers, then real unity is impossible.

Working-class unity is not something to be proclaimed by ignoring racism, xenophobia, and other oppressions within the working class, but something to fight for by combatting them. Some critics of socialism claim that we prioritize class struggle over issues like racism and sexism. In fact, we see them as inseparable. Of course, some socialists have screwed up this question—and many others. But most have a proud history of fighting oppression. In the 1930s, for example, thousands of members of the American Communist Party did pathbreaking and courageous work against segregation in the South. It was so effective that for decades afterward antiracism and communism were viewed synonymously by southern bigots, who called civil rights activists "communists" and communists "n****r lovers."[6]

Socialists aim to win workers to fight against oppression on the basis not of sympathy but of solidarity, the idea that this fight is in

---

5. There's a special circle in lefty hell reserved for activists who dismiss the importance of oppressions they don't even experience. Perhaps an eternal planning meeting with a bunch of men getting repeatedly flicked in the balls while the devil yells at them to stop being distracted and "focus on the real issues."

6. A couple of great books about some of the Communists' antiracist work in the 1930s are *Hammer and Hoe* by Robin D. G. Kelley and *Communists in Harlem* by Mark Naison. For a more general look at the history of socialists and the Black struggle in the United States, read *Black Liberation and Socialism* by Ahmed Shawki.

mutual working-class interests. Here is how Eugene Debs, the greatest socialist in US history, put it when he stood before a court that had convicted him of speaking out against the First World War: "Your Honor, years ago I recognized my kinship with all living beings, and I made up my mind that I was not one bit better than the meanest on earth. I said then, and I say now, that while there is a lower class, I am in it, and while there is a criminal element I am of it, and while there is a soul in prison, I am not free."

Beautiful words, but they are only remembered because Debs backed them up every day of his life.[7] Solidarity is an idea, but it is also something that takes time to build, a network of relationships based on the trust that if I stand up, you will have my back. The recent British movie *Pride*, about the connections built between London LGBT activists and coal miners during their epic 1984–85 strike, details the slow process of how solidarity was forged between two groups that initially viewed each other with distrust and ignorance. It begins with a small handful of LGBT activists—many of whom had radical politics and working-class backgrounds—trying to find a miners union local that would accept donations from a group that called itself "Lesbians and Gays Support the Miners," which wasn't easy back in the mid-1980s. When they did find a willing union in Wales, they showed their sincerity by raising serious money and support for the strike in the gay community and driving out to Wales for regular picket line visits. A year later, the miners made the return drive to London to march alongside their new comrades in the Gay Pride Parade, which gives the movie a nice Hollywood ending[8] that happens to be completely true.

---

7. For a short intro about Debs, look up Howard Zinn's "Eugene Debs and the Idea of Socialism."

8. Except for the miners' strike going down to crushing defeat and the leading activist dying of AIDS. Spoiler alert: the eighties sucked.

Working-class solidarity against oppression is possible because all workers experience oppression, although they may not always feel it in their daily lives. As the Polish socialist Rosa Luxemburg once said: "Those who do not move do not notice their chains." At home on the couch, workers are just as likely as anyone else to buy whatever crappy ideas this society is selling. When they find themselves in a struggle, they make connections between themselves and others facing injustice. Some white workers begin to think about how the way management harasses them for no reason is similar to what Black people face from the police—and management.

In the early nineties there was a three-year strike in southern Illinois at the Staley corn sweetener factory. As the strike went on, many workers grew frustrated with their union's lack of a strategy and started going out on their own to build community support. When Black workers organized a contingent in the local Martin Luther King Jr. Day parade, dozens of their white coworkers joined them, the first time almost any of them had participated in an MLK Day event. Within a few months, they were organizing a march to commemorate King's assassination, chanting "Black and white, united we fight!" These white workers from rural Illinois might have initially reached out to Black organizations simply to build support for their strike, but they came away from the experience understanding that the fights for labor rights and civil rights are connected.

"It's not the struggle for flat-screen TVs that motivates white unionized workers and a fight for dignity and justice that drives low-wage Black and immigrant workers," writes union activist Amy Muldoon. "There is a longing for justice throughout the working majority in society that goes unnamed as long as our identity as working-class people and the oppression we suffer as a consequence is hidden." We are living through a time when the number of strikes and the size of unions is at a historically low level. Its not just the oppression of the working class that's hidden—so is its power. So it isn't surprising that many people looking to fight oppression and injustice find that the idea that the workers will lead the way outdated and naïve.

Even the phrase *working class* seems to be old-fashioned, as if it referred to an ancient race of white, male factory workers with overalls and lunch buckets. I write for and distribute a newspaper called *Socialist Worker*, whose title dates back to the late 1970s when lots of radical papers were called things like that. Today the name can seem moldy—not the *Socialist* part, but the *Worker*. Which is ridiculous, because most people continue to be workers. You don't have to work in a car factory to be a worker (although a certain number of people still do, which is why we have cars). You can work in an office building or a Chipotle. You don't have to be a white man to be a worker, and in fact you never did.

It's true that the working class has undergone major changes. Within the United States, factory work has shifted from northern cities to rural areas, especially in the South and West. Some blue-collar jobs have been replaced by machines, just as the San Francisco CEO hoped would happen to his city's transit workers. But let's not exaggerate these trends. The global working class is bigger than it has ever been. What is often called deindustrialization is really a process in which factory jobs haven't disappeared but relocated to places without unions in the United States and around the world. It's funny how many professors and newspaper columnists use their factory-made laptops to write about our deindustrialized world, and then email those words for publication through fiber-optic cables that are also made in factories. If these writers would just look outside their office windows, they might even notice those cables being installed or repaired by good old-fashioned workers—wearing hard hats no less! Even in the United States, there are still plenty of industrial workers, and they produce more than ever, which means they can disrupt more than ever. Meanwhile, millions of workers in nonindustrial fields like health care and retail have seen their jobs start to resemble factory work as their companies import the "Toyota business model" to increase worker productivity.

One reason the working class doesn't seem present in the way it used to be is that class is not just a statistic but also an awareness. As workers come together to fight in their own interest, Marx once wrote, they change from being a class "in itself" to one that is consciously "for itself." Conversely, when working-class unions and parties are weak, workers' voices disappear from public conversation as if they don't exist.

In the early seventies the US media frequently covered a trend they dubbed "blue-collar blues": young workers influenced by the protest movements of the sixties who were sick and tired of the bleak world of factory life. The mood was epitomized by a 1972 strike by autoworkers in Lordstown, Ohio, where the main issue wasn't money or benefits but assembly-line speedups. The local union leader said that his members were striking for the right to be "able to smoke, bullshit a bit, open a book, daydream even."[9]

Nobody talks about blue-collar blues anymore, even though factory conditions haven't changed for the better. Here is how a current autoworker describes conditions at his job:

> We're an ultra-lean production facility, which means we run with as few people as possible on the floor . . . we don't have people to give bathroom breaks. . . . You feel like if I do this anymore I will

9. The story is covered in Studs Terkel's oral history collection *Working*. Can you imagine a strike like that today? "No Facebook? No Peace!"

go fucking insane. And then you go fucking insane but then you just keep doing it. And it's like your life is a continual stream of insanity because you're a robot. That's what they make you into.

The conditions haven't changed, but the level of resistance has—for the worse. The speaker is not on strike and he is not talking to a reporter. He is at a meeting at the 2013 Socialism conference, one of the few places interested in giving workers a platform. As far as the general media is concerned, autoworkers should be thrilled to still have a job.

But the decline in the power of workers, like their numbers, is easily exaggerated. Pundits regularly dismiss unions as insignificant relics of the past, until a strike erupts and they freak out about how much chaos it will cause. Even then, they are often incapable of actually listening to the workers they now realize they depend on. "Get 'em back to work, pay them whatever they want, and then figure out how to automate their jobs so this doesn't happen again." The tech boss assumes the transit workers are striking for more money, but their key issue is to maintain work rules that give them a say over job assignments. They want some of the same autonomy that any CEO would expect as a given. Most labor disputes are as much about dignity as they are about pay. This rarely comes across in news coverage that is bent on portraying striking workers as greedy for putting their own interests ahead of customers who may be inconvenienced by a strike.

In fact, US labor laws make it illegal for most workers to strike over issues that affect customers, other workers, or the general public.[10]

---

10. The Taft-Hartley law from 1947 bars workers from striking against anyone other than their direct employer. After the law was passed by a Republican Congress, Harry Truman and the Democrats campaigned the next year on a promise to overturn the law. The labor movement mobilized its members to vote, reelected Truman, won Democratic majorities in both the House and Senate, and . . . we still have Taft-Hartley. Truman himself used it twelve times to break strikes in his second term.

Yet for some reason, the press and politicians who scold unions for only looking out for themselves never call for changing laws to allow them to go on strike for others. When Chicago teachers struck in 2012, some of their main concerns were the city's huge class sizes and deteriorating school buildings. The mayor told them that those weren't legal bargaining issues—and then denounced them for not caring about the children.

A few months after the BART strike, transit workers at the Long Island Rail Road in New York threatened to walk out, sending political and business leaders into a tizzy. What really baffled them was that the workers were not upset about their own pay and benefits but about proposed cuts for future hires. This principle of fighting for future workers is widely understood by union members, who call it "protecting the unborn"—which we can only hope even further infuriates those in management who are also anti-abortion. But it's a foreign and therefore infuriating concept for bankers, bosses, and even many bloggers who have never experienced collective labor. The idea of workers sacrificing today's wages for the sake of preserving a standard of living for people they don't even know tomorrow strikes them as crazy.

That's why these are exactly the people who shouldn't be in charge of making long-term decisions about our planet. The working class could do a much better job, not the class as it exists right now but the one that can come into being through future struggles. Socialists aim to help that process along, by providing a platform for workers' voices and keeping alive the lessons and spirit of the times when workers have built unions, overthrown governments, and dared to strike for the right to bullshit, daydream, and read a book.

As Michael Zweig writes:

> The capitalist class . . . has created institutions vital to its reproduction as a class and the stability of its ruling class, including

elite educational institutions, social clubs, and business, trade, and lobbying groups. . . . The working class is also reproduced across generations through the institutions and media representations that working people encounter, some of their own making, most not. . . . But, unlike the capitalist and ruling classes, the working class has no institutions designed to forge it into a social force ready to give strategic guidance to society.

Socialists aim to create those institutions, not just by preserving the legacy of the working class but also by joining and giving shape to the new fights that capitalists just can't help themselves from provoking, from fast-food worker strikes to young immigrants publicly declaring themselves "undocumented and unafraid" to the car plant that doesn't let its worker-bots go to the bathroom, which saw its production lines get shut down for hours when a handful of workers decided they'd had enough.[11] Most of these fights are small. Ideally, there would be massive protests happening all the time. But the working class inherently finds itself at a disadvantage. Terry Eagleton finds an analogy to our current situation in an old Irish joke about someone who is asked the way about to the railroad station and responds, "Well I wouldn't start from here." Socialists, Eagleton says, might feel the same way about today's low level of class struggle. "But there is, of course, nowhere else to start from. A different future has to be the future of this particular present."

But how do we get from this particular present to socialism? How can tens of millions of workers become revolutionary? Through a revolution. That might seem like it gets the chronology wrong. We're taught to view revolutions as the final step of a plan carried

---

11. You can listen to the talk about what's happening in auto plants today at WeAreMany.org. Look up "The New Fightback in Auto."

out by radical leaders, when in fact they are the process by which millions of ordinary people become radical leaders. But then so much that we learn about revolutions is backwards. It probably would take a whole chapter of a book to set things right. Fortunately . . .

8.

Revolution!

In our culture of shameless self-promotion, the word *revolution* is used so often that it loses any meaning.[1] Advertisements boast about revolutionary advancements in four-wheel drive, stain removal, and getting a close, clean shave. Executives are lauded for revolutionizing the human experience by enabling us to buy our deodorant online. But amid the constant barrage of corporate hype, we sometimes catch snippets of actual revolutions in faraway countries: people facing off in the streets against dictators armed with high-tech weaponry purchased from the same rich countries where billboards urge the citizenry to talk to their doctors about how to *Join the Revolution* against erectile dysfunction. Real revolutions, the tone of the newscasters says, are not cool or cutting edge at all, but frightening echoes from humanity's bad old days.

Socialists view revolutions quite differently. We recognize their scary and tragic elements, but we also see the wonder and amazement

---

1. Just like *genius, once in a lifetime*, and *World's Greatest Cup of Coffee!*

of millions of people realizing for the first time some of the incredible powers they possess when they act in unity. Revolutions are the fullest expression of social life, when the majority of the population pushes away its self-appointed spokespeople and demands to make itself heard. To reject in advance the path of revolution out of fear of the possible consequences is the political equivalent of living a lonely and risk-free life in order to avoid pain and rejection.

If all this sounds a bit romantic, that's because it is. Socialists are hopeless romantics—or at least they should be. We love people and think that ordinary human beings (including ourselves) are in fact extraordinary, and revolutions are the only time that most of them get to show it—to the world and to themselves. It's been almost half a century since the 1960s, when the last great revolutionary wave swept the world from the slums of Algiers to the factories of Paris and Detroit.[2] Entire generations since then have grown up cynical about political romance. The fabulous sixties slogan "Be realistic, demand the impossible" has been replaced by self-help mantras about sticking to what you can control and not making demands of anybody but yourself.

Then revolutions broke out in 2011 across North Africa and the Middle East, millions who had suffocated for decades under monarchies and military dictatorships took over city plazas and refused to be moved, and romantic feelings that had long been dormant were rekindled. People everywhere were touched by the Arab Spring and inspired by the sudden transformation of what had been the most rigidly unchanged region of the globe.

---

2. Three quick recommendations: Gille Pontecorvo's intense movie *The Battle of Algiers* about the Algerian revolution to win independence from France; Daniel Singer's *Prelude to Revolution* about the French general strike in 1968; Dan Georgakis and Marvin Surkin's *Detroit, I Do Mind Dying* about the League of Revolutionary Black Workers.

But the regimes struck back and new counterrevolutionary forces like ISIS emerged. The uprisings were drowned in military repression in Egypt and Bahrain and civil war in Syria and Libya. Many in the Middle East and beyond now question whether the revolution actually happened or if it was just a mirage. It is just that question that every counterrevolution in history has aimed to produce. Revolutions are not a single event but a process, which unfortunately involves many defeats, some of which are decisive and last decades, while others prove to be more temporary setbacks. Whichever of these is true about the Arab Spring—and I'm guessing the latter—it has already accomplished the important task of showing a new generation that revolution can be more than advertising filler.

What Exactly Is a Revolutionary?

Growing up I never would have thought that I would become a revolutionary—and that's certainly not the way I would normally describe myself. Revolutionaries are supposed to march in the jungle in camo fatigues, while I'm chilling on a couch wearing my comfy pajama pants.[3] I don't have the personality you might associate with someone looking to upend the political system: I've never been in a fistfight, and I generally try to avoid confrontation in my personal life. But I am a revolutionary, not because of the way I dress, talk, or behave but because I believe there needs to be a revolution, and I do my best to act on those beliefs.

Before I became a socialist I thought that revolutionaries were people who would rather stand on the sidelines making radical speeches (or smoking weed) than get involved in the often years-long

---

3. No, they're not footie pajamas. Those actually might be grounds for disqualification from the revolution.

fights to win small but important changes like raising the minimum wage. I didn't actually know any revolutionaries, but I was pretty confident in my assessment based on an extensive exposure to Hollywood movies about the sixties and goofy radical sitcom characters. It turns out that being a revolutionary doesn't at all mean rejecting the fight for reforms—my comrades and I have spent years fighting for causes as diverse as ending the death penalty, winning marriage equality, and getting more funding for local schools. What we do reject is something called reformism, which is the idea that we can not only win various reforms to make capitalism a little better for a little while but that by passing more and more progressive laws we can slowly but surely reform capitalism itself into a system that works for the majority of humanity. Reformism is an appealing strategy because it seems a lot more practical than revolution. The problem is that if your goal is socialism, reformism doesn't work.

Socialism can't be gradually voted into existence. Democracy under capitalism doesn't even cover such basic questions as whether a local private hospital should be closed or whether we should be bombarded with sexist ads using women's bodies to sell products, so we're certainly not going to be allowed to vote on whether or not to abolish the profit system. "I don't see why we need to stand by and watch a country go communist because of the irresponsibility of its own people." Those were the words of US Secretary of State Henry Kissinger in 1970 when Chile elected the Socialist Party to run the government. Within three years, the CIA and Chilean military had overthrown the democratic government and murdered tens of thousands of its supporters.

Even if it were possible to elect socialist leaders across the world to disband armies, end poverty, and declare that Mardi Gras will now be held every Wednesday, the creation of socialist societies might still require revolutions. It is only through the experiences of revolution that millions of workers go through the learning process necessary to run society. Or, as Marx once put it: "We say to the workers you will have to go through years of civil wars not only in order to change conditions but in order to change yourselves." This sounds a little more grim to modern ears than Marx may have intended. By "civil wars," he was not necessarily referring to military battles but intense conflicts between classes that could take many forms—from workplace occupations to creating new constitutions to street battles with police or soldiers. These conflicts can involve not just pain and loss but the exhilaration of discovering previously unknown capacities and skills—as individuals, as a class, and as a society. Still, there's no getting around the fact that years of struggle is more of a bummer than peaceful elections and Mardi Gras Wednesdays.

Of course, revolutions don't just happen whenever revolutionaries want them to—the very nature of a revolution is that it's an uprising of far larger numbers of people than the minority who are normally down for revolution. I don't recommend standing outside the White House tomorrow with a megaphone demanding that the government surrender. So what do revolutionaries do in "normal," nonrevolutionary times? Some activists view being a revolutionary as a personal statement—they show up at protests wanting to do the most radical thing possible, like blocking traffic or breaking a store window, whether or not it makes sense in that moment, because it's an expression of how they feel about the system.

For socialists, being a revolutionary is not a state of mind, a style of protest, or what clique you sit with in the school cafeteria. Instead it's about understanding that capitalism inevitably produces revolutions and doing what you can to prepare for them so that they might win—the tricky part being that you don't know if that scenario might arise in five years or fifty. Preparing for revolution doesn't mean stocking up on canned food and flashlights.[4] It means training ourselves and those who join us for the future—by reading and discussing the lessons of the past and fighting and learning how to win in the protest movements of the present.

We spend much of our time in these various movements working alongside reformists inside unions, nonprofit organizations, and activist coalitions—which often leads to debates. Most reformists in the United States think the only realistic strategy to win gradual change is to stay inside the Democratic Party and make it more progressive from the inside, whereas most revolutionaries think that people fighting for things like racial, gender, and class equality should be independent of a party that doesn't share those goals and that we should aim to one day build a new party based on more radical demands. The differences between moderates and radicals can even extend to having different approaches for organizing a meeting. Many reformists prefer to keep meetings focused on practical tasks and view open-ended political discussions as an "unproductive" use of time. Revolutionaries, by contrast, want to make sure there's time for political discussions so that people can explore new perspectives they're gaining from their experience in the movement. Most people who go to a protest or find themselves on strike are not necessarily opposed to the entire capitalist system. Yet once they step outside the path of their daily commute and engage in resistance—no matter how minor—they often begin to see life from a different angle.

Perhaps the local news distorts important details about the demonstration you were just on. How can you not wonder what other

---

4. That's actually preparing for the increasing number of megastorms we face from increased climate change that will only get worse if we don't have a revolution.

stories they are lying to us about? Or maybe you're out on strike when some coworkers stop chanting to leer at a woman walking past the picket line. Their everyday sexism didn't used to get to you that much because it was part of the daily bullshit of being at work, but now that you're in a serious fight for your health care it strikes you as so much more demeaning. You start thinking about the other sexism you've always put up with because it doesn't bother you "too much." You explain all this to your coworkers in a few choice words, and a few of them listen a little more closely than they normally would because they know they need everyone to stick together to win the strike.

Even the briefest experience of resisting exploitation or oppression can be a life-altering moment, like finally discovering what it feels like to breathe clean air after a lifetime of pollution. A few years ago two hundred and fifty UPS workers walked off the job in response to an unjust firing. After a long fight, the fired driver got his job back, but the two hundred and fifty who walked out for him each lost ten days' pay. Most of them took it as a victory, which speaks volumes about the meaning of solidarity. I reported on the story for *Socialist Worker*[5] and got to know one of the workers pretty well. Those two hundred and fifty guys didn't just walk out for the fired driver, he said. "They walked out for themselves. For those ninety minutes we were out there in the parking lot, we felt freedom." He was talking at a socialist meeting, a place he might never have imagined himself being a few months earlier. But the experience of the walkout and fight afterward to save the jobs had changed his worldview. A few weeks later he told me that unions, when you think about it, are basically a communist effort at their heart. Unlike Fox News, he meant it as a compliment.

---

5. It was one of those times that the name of the paper seemed just fine.

In revolutionary situations, that change in perspective of one UPS worker happens to millions of working-class people as they experience what power feels like for the first time and begin to process what that means about the entire lives they have been living and what it could mean for the lives they will lead afterward. In *Prelude to Revolution*, Daniel Singer described the profound psychological impact of the events in Paris in May 1968, when students took over the streets and workers went on the largest strike the world had ever seen.

> When the productive machine grinds to a halt, the cogs themselves begin wondering about their function. When there is no gasoline, when public transport has come to a halt, when there is no smoke coming out of the factory's chimney, no normal work in the office, when the usual rhythm of social life has broken down, can the human mind alone stick to the routine? Do you remember those rare sleepless nights when, lying uncomfortably awake, you vividly recollect the hopes or illusions of youth and set this promise against the fulfillment, when with painful lucidity you ponder the meaning of your life? Something of that kind all at once happens to thousands, and it happens during the day. Only this collective blues is coupled with collective hope, is really inspired by it. The prospect of change releases the inner censorship. It prompts one to confess that the present is intolerable, to admit it to oneself but also to others. In factories, in offices, groups gather to discuss what can be done.

This is the beginning of a revolutionary situation, a joyous and disorienting mass feeling that's happened many times and in many places. The danger is that while the regular people are out in the streets having conversations for the first time since they were kids about what the world should look like, the people who are usually in charge of those matters are plotting how to bring things back to normal as soon as possible. For the working class to realize its potential in this situation to take control of society, there needs to be a large socialist party with deep roots among workers that can fight to give a definite direction in this exhilarating atmosphere of open-ended possibility. It's only happened once.

Time to Talk about Russia

The short version of the 1917 Russian Revolution that most of us learn goes something like this: The Russian people were angry about being poor and being sent to die in a miserable war by their incompetent tsar (that's what the Russian king was called). This anger was skillfully manipulated by the Bolshevik Party and their crafty leader Vladimir Lenin in order to create a revolution that gave the Bolsheviks absolute power to impose their fanatical socialist ideals on the country, leading to decades of misery under Lenin's sidekick Joseph Stalin.

This story gets two things right: the angry people in the beginning and the misery under Stalin after the revolution was defeated. But there's some stuff in between—very interesting stuff in which millions of Russian workers, peasants, and soldiers formed the largest democratic bodies in history, created the beginnings of a new type of society the world had never seen, and inspired workers in dozens of countries to form their own Communist parties—that are left out of the picture.[6] This middle part gets cut out because it gets in the way of hammering home the lessons we're meant to take from the

---

6. There are a million good books written about the Russian Revolution and a zillion—sorry, a shlazillion—bad ones. The most profound and most beautifully written one I know of is Leon Trotsky's *History of the Russian Revolution*. It's also 1,200 pages and presumes you already know some of the history. A good introductory article is "80 Years Since the Russian Revolution" by Ahmed Shawki.

Russian Revolution: that socialism can't work, power always corrupts, and everyday people who join revolutions are just dupes being manipulated by one or another group of elites.

People have good reason to be suspicious that socialists intend to simply use workers as an army to overturn capitalism and then turn on them once in power. History is filled with examples of rebellions that end with the masses being betrayed by the leaders they put into power. This is true to an extent even of genuinely important revolutions such as the one that created the United States of America. The American Revolution overthrew British colonialism and monarchy and created one of the world's first modern democracies. The Declaration of Independence's proclamation that all men are created equal inspired revolutionaries around the world—or at least those who had Y chromosomes. But within a few years of independence came Shays' Rebellion, an uprising of poor Massachusetts farmers who had fought in the revolution (often without being paid) and now were being thrown into jail when they couldn't pay their debts. The response of the new country's leaders—almost all of whom were wealthy landowners—was not to address the concerns of the people who had sacrificed so much in fighting the British but to instead create a new thing called the Constitution to give them a stronger central government and army that could more quickly put down future rebellions of the poor. Plus, you know, slavery. The charge that many a good American patriot has leveled at the Bolsheviks—that they used the revolutionary masses for their own gain—applies far more accurately to his revered Founding Fathers than to Lenin and his comrades. In fact, the real reason the Bolsheviks have been demonized for the past hundred years is that they did precisely the opposite—they pushed the revolution past the initial stage of a new elite taking control to a more radical transformation of society in which power really was in the hands of the masses of people.

The first thing to understand about the Russian Revolution is that there was not one revolution but two: the overthrow of the tsar in February and the creation of a soviet government in October. The February revolution was not planned by Lenin—or anybody else. It exploded mostly spontaneously after a strike of women clothing workers spread across the capital city—with the help of the Bolsheviks and other socialists—and snowballed into an unstoppable force that within days forced the tsar to step down and created a new provisional (or temporary) government. This first revolution had features shared by the initial days of many other revolutions: unpredictability, a joyous disbelief that a regime that had been all-powerful for so long could be overthrown so easily, and a leading role played by working women. When large numbers of working-class women, who normally are too burdened by daily responsibilities to lead protests, start showing up, things are about to get serious.

The first Provisional Government was dominated by parties from the wealthy landowning and capitalist classes, which is also not unusual. After a tyrant is overthrown, the initial government to replace it often contains people who for the most part supported the old regime but now claim to have always been on the side of the people. At this early stage many of the people are okay with that. They are carried away by the beautiful unity that toppled the tyrant and still think it natural for those with the most money, status, and education to run society. In these early days different classes can celebrate together without taking up the inevitable question of who will be in charge of the store once everybody goes back to work. Factory workers and factory owners who will soon be at each other's throats can toast together the fall of the king.

But after a week or two of widespread public partying and hugging strangers in the street the way folks tend to do after they've overthrown a thousand-year-old dictatorship, the people of Russia were confronted with the question of what to do next. The whole country agreed—or at least claimed to agree—that there should be a democratic government. But beyond that loomed huge disagreements. Poor peasants—the majority of the country—wanted land. Industrial workers and their families wanted a shorter workday and an end to food shortages. Wealthy business and landowners, not surprisingly, had other ideas. Meanwhile, both peasants and workers wanted Russia to pull out of World War I, which had already killed more than a million and a half Russian soldiers. But Russia's powerful allies England and France needed Russia to keep fighting, and the business and landowners depended on those allies for loans and political support.

For the elites in charge of the Provisional Government, democracy meant having an elected government—someday; they kept putting off the elections—that would maintain the tsar's policies, most importantly continuing the war. As Americans we are very familiar with this version of democracy—the kind where no matter whom you elect the One Percent always remains in charge. But the Provisional Government's plans were challenged by new organizations created by the revolution called soviets, councils of elected representatives that started in the factories of the capital and then spread among workers, peasants, soldiers, students, women, neighborhoods, and villages. These soviets controlled the post office, railroads, and food distribution in the capital city, and as the year went on, their influence spread across the country. Military officers on the front could not even have their orders carried out without the approval of the soldiers' council, which put a crimp in the army's go-to strategy of sending wave after wave of poor peasant soldiers to certain death.[7]

Since the soviets were performing many of the functions of government—in a radically more democratic way—the Bolsheviks argued that they could and should become the new government and begin the construction of a socialist society. Not surprisingly, Russia's upper classes weren't big fans of this plan, but neither were the two other socialist parties, which had a reformist approach that the revolution needed to limit itself to creating a democratic government led by capitalists, because economically backward Russia had a working class that was too small and underdeveloped to take power. Only many years later, they argued, would a socialist revolution be possible. The Bolsheviks agreed that it would be impossible for socialism to develop in Russia alone, but they believed that the example of a successful workers' revolution in Russia could inspire similar revolutions in countries like Germany, where greater economic resources and a larger and more powerful working class could make socialism a reality.

The Bolsheviks were a minority force at the beginning of the revolution, but that changed as the year went on and the Provisional Government continued to find new excuses for not meeting the demands of workers and peasants, most of which began with "as soon as we win this war." Through months of stormy protests, strikes, peasant uprisings, and army mutinies, the Bolsheviks grew from a few thousand based among the most radical factory workers to an organization of hundreds of thousands based in many workplaces and throughout the army and navy. When in August a right-wing

---

7. Many Russian soldiers were sent into battle without boots—which come in particularly handy in freaking Russia—or guns, which have also been known to be useful on the battlefield. But please remember that it's Lenin and the Bolsheviks who were the heartless tyrants.

general named Kornilov tried to launch a coup and the hapless Provisional Government didn't know what to do, it was the Bolshevik-influenced soviets of railroad and telegraph workers who stopped him. Bolshevik leader Leon Trotsky later described how they did it in his classic *History of the Russian Revolution:*

> The railroad workers in those days did their duty. In a mysterious way echelons [of Kornilov's troops] would find themselves moving on the wrong roads. Regiments would arrive in the wrong division, artillery would be sent up a blind alley, staffs would get out of communication with their units. All the big stations had their own Soviets, their railroad workers' and their military committees. The telegraphers kept them informed of all events, all movements, all changes. The telegraphers also held up the orders of Kornilov. . . . It was in this atmosphere that the Kornilov echelons advanced—or what was worse, stood still.

By the fall, Bolsheviks had been elected to the majority of the citywide soviets in the capital city, and party leaders were publicly debating each other in newspaper columns over whether and how to take power from the official government. When they finally did in October, the move was so widely supported that there were almost no soldiers in the capital who defended the official government, although the fighting in other cities lasted for a few weeks.

While the majority of Russian workers supported the October revolution, the more moderate socialist parties rejected it on the grounds that it was not democratic because it hadn't been elected, a detail they hadn't found objectionable in February when the tsar was overthrown without a formal vote having taken place. Their accusation that the October revolution was a tyrannical turn against the "democratic" February revolution has been echoed by most historians, so it's worth a response. The fact is that every revolution happens without a vote: If the change people are looking for could happen within the election process, there would be no need to revolt. Just as a revolution was necessary in February because a democracy couldn't be created under the tsar's monarchy, another one was necessary in October because soviets couldn't take power and create a far more democratic government under the direct control of the working masses while the Provisional Government controlled (or tried to control) the army, police, and other wings of the state. A revolution is usually initiated by a minority, but it can only succeed if that minority can win the support of the majority, which is what occurred both in February and in October.

Over the course of 1917 the Russian working class had, as Marx described, both changed the conditions of the country and changed itself through its creation of and participation in the soviets. Workers supported the October revolution not because they were manipulated by the Bolshevik Party but because they came to agree with its strategies and theory through their own experience of power and self-organization.

What then happened after the October revolution was the exact opposite of a small party seizing power for itself. The first acts of the new soviet government were directed toward giving workers control of the factories and peasants control of the land—not through strict government control but through their own actions. These decrees called on the soviets and other popular committees of workers and peasants to take over the land and factories themselves. The Bolsheviks were using their control of the government to create a new kind of state based on people taking power for themselves.

Within weeks, the soviet government had called for an immediate end to Russia's participation in the war and legalized divorce, abortion, and homosexuality—narrowly beating the United States on these progressive reforms by around fifty years or so. It also declared that nations controlled by the tsar's empire had the right to declare independence and embarrassed Russia's "democratic" allies England and France by publishing their secret plans to divide up the colonial territories of their enemies after the war. The world had never seen a government like this, with the combined boldness of Occupy Wall Street, Pussy Riot, and WikiLeaks.[8]

While all this was taking place in Russia, the revolutionary wave did indeed spread elsewhere, as the Bolsheviks had hoped. Two months after the October revolution, Germany was shut down by a weeklong strike that called for immediate peace with Russia, in addition to raising German workers' own economic demands. A year later came a full revolution, which included the creation of German workers' soviets. But the German socialist movement was dominated by the same type of moderates who rejected the October revolution in Russia. Like their Russian counterparts, the German moderates argued that the country wasn't ready for workers to take direct power. Unlike their Russian counterparts, they were able to use their authority in the new government to disband the soviets, repress the revolutionary workers, and murder the radical leaders Rosa Luxemburg and Karl Liebknecht. Apparently that's the democratic way to have a revolution.

There were more uprisings to come in Germany and elsewhere, but no successful revolutions, which made the eventual failure of the Russian Revolution inevitable, as the Bolsheviks knew. They had always said that socialism couldn't succeed if it was isolated in Russia—

---

8. Contrast these lightning changes to the presidency of Barack Obama, who took three years just to end the military's "don't ask don't tell" policy toward gay soldiers. When his spokesperson was asked what was taking so long, the response was that the president "has a lot on his plate." Must be a slow eater.

and that was before the country was wrecked by World War I and then invaded by foreign powers after the revolution. In the years after 1917, workers in Russian cities faced starvation, while peasants were furious that the new government they had fought for was now taking their bread to feed the workers. As workers lost their strength and organization, real authority shifted from soviets to the bureaucracy of the Bolshevik government. Many peasants turned against the revolution and led uprisings that were suppressed. Leaders like Lenin and Trotsky publicly worried that the popular character of the revolution was deteriorating and urged government officials to maintain as much democratic culture as possible while waiting for new revolutions to break out in other countries and relieve Russia's isolation. It's a testament to the inspirational power of the revolution that, even during these troubled years in the 1920s, Russia saw artistic explosions in cinema and graphic design, breakthroughs in psychology, and a sexual revolution that reached deep into the countryside.[9]

But some prominent Bolsheviks, led by Joseph Stalin, concluded that if the revolution wasn't going to spread, it would be better to survive in power by creating an autocracy than to wait to be overthrown by foreign armies and the old Russian ruling classes. Stalin maneuvered his way into a dictatorship and launched a historic reign of terror, featuring slave labor camps and mass executions of political enemies. Every gain of the revolution was reversed: art and writing were rigorously censored, homosexuality and abortion were criminalized again, and women were told that being a good communist meant having lots of children for Mother Russia.

Stalin, a longtime dedicated Bolshevik turned ruthless tyrant, is the poster child for the commonsense idea that power inevitably

---

9. Don't worry. We'll come back to peasant sex in chapter 10.

corrupts. But to say that a revolution that saw tens of millions participating in mass soviet democracy became a monstrous dictatorship because of one man's ruthless thirst for power is a nursery-rhyme version of history, like saying the American Revolution succeeded because George Washington was so honest about chopping down that cherry tree. The defeat from within of the Soviet Union was a decade-long process in which the soviets stopped functioning in conditions of war and mass poverty and the Bolshevik Party was left in charge of a state presiding over a devastated economy. As the party had to make more and more emergency decisions—often with the fate of the revolution on the line—the revolutionary dynamic of the people fighting for their own liberation completely shifted to a small number of ex-revolutionaries fighting for their own position as the leaders of the country. The outcome of the Russian Revolution is a confirmation of the basic Marxist idea that socialism has to come from the workers themselves. But it was convenient both for Stalin and his fellow "communist" leaders and for their enemies in the "free world" to assert the opposite—that this new type of dictatorship ruling in the name of the people was what "actually existing socialism" looked like in practice.

Powerlessness Isn't Empowering

Revolutionary workers' councils similar to the ones in Russia and Germany have reappeared in Spain in 1936, Hungary in 1956, Chile in 1972, Iran in 1978, and Poland in 1981. As in Russia between February and October 1917, the existence of these councils created the potential for a situation known as dual power, in which the normal authority of government is challenged—although not always consciously—by these new workers' organizations. Situations of dual power are unstable and cannot last for very long. The Bolsheviks used the eight months of dual power to organize support for the so-viets to take over. No major party in these later revolutions did the same, and in each case the government was able to take back control, disband the councils, and roll back the revolution.

Something had changed in the revolutionary socialist movement since the Russian Revolution, and that something was the Russian Revolution itself. After taking over the Bolshevik Party and government, Stalin and his allies manipulated the loyalty of the Communist parties that had formed around the world in 1917, handpicked new leaders who would blindly obey Moscow, and turned the primary function of these once-revolutionary parties into being cheerleaders for Russian foreign policy—which is not to say that they didn't do important work building unions and other protest movements. The result was that in subsequent revolutions, Communist parties played the same role that the moderate socialists had played in Russia, arguing that the working class was not ready to take power. Or, as in the case of Hungary and Poland, which were part of the Eastern European bloc of regimes created by Stalin at the end of World War II, the Communist parties themselves were the despised one-party state that the workers were trying to overthrow. The tragic outcome of the Russian Revolution and the Communist parties it inspired has cast a shadow over every subsequent generation attempting to challenge capitalism. It has become widely accepted that working-class revolution is not possible or desirable—even among those who consider themselves anticapitalist revolutionaries. If that seems like a contradiction, some radicals get around it by redefining revolution to mean, as the title of one influential book puts it, to "Change the World without Taking Power."

"What is a revolution?" asks the anarchist David Graeber. "We used to think we knew. Revolutions were seizures of power by popular forces aiming to transform the very nature of the political, social, and economic system in the country in which the revolution took place." Today, he goes on to say, revolutionaries understand that the most important transformations are those like the feminist movement of the 1960s and 1970s that permanently changed society without any governments falling. Graeber makes the valuable points that feminists and other activists who devoted their lives to struggle have not done so in vain and that the profound effects they have had on our lives are no less important just because capitalism is still standing. But that doesn't mean we should drop the goal of transforming social, political, and economic systems, which need to be transformed more than ever. The fact that they haven't is the reason why the gains made by feminism are in danger of being undermined by a system that continues to rely on women's unpaid labor in the home and uses their bodies to sell products. Then there's the issue of climate change, which has no solution that doesn't involve taking the world's decision-making authority away from a class that can't stop itself from endangering the prospects of human life on Earth because it has too much invested in an economy based on fossil fuel. Taking power still needs to be on the agenda.

That's why debates about the Russian Revolution continue to resonate among socialists and others on the left, even though the conditions we face today look nothing like those in a mostly peasant country a century ago. The key point is not whether every Bolshevik idea or action was right or wrong—although there is much to be learned from those details—but whether they were right to attempt to lead the workers' councils into the quest for power. Some people find this bizarre or pathetic, as if we are the political equivalent of fantasy enthusiasts who put on jester costumes and go to Renaissance Fairs. There are legitimate reasons to laugh at socialists, believe me, but this isn't one of them. Revolutions may be rare, but they're not random. Each one has so much to teach us because they reveal deep truths about capitalist society that normally are hidden. Scientists study tectonic earthquakes not only to predict when future earthquakes can occur but also because they are rare opportunities to study the interaction of plates that normally can't be observed because they are grinding away deep under the surface of the planet. So it is with revolutions and social classes. Workers are usually so busy being exploited and oppressed that they appear to have little interest in the major political questions of the day, much less the ability to solve them. But the seismic shift of revolution reveals that the class has more depth than was visible from the surface. Suddenly workers are intensely debating every aspect of how society is run and using their new committees and councils to act decisively on those debates. At the same time, the bosses who just yesterday were unquestioned leaders now stand naked in their powerlessness before the world, because their workers are no longer following their orders. All the while, middle-class leaders who used to confidently think they represented all of society career desperately back and forth between whichever of the two contending classes seems to offer a way out of a conflict in which they can only see chaos.

Those who focus only on the chaos and violence of revolutions imply that there is a peaceful democratic alternative. But revolutions occur precisely because there isn't. They are emergency measures taken spontaneously by large numbers of people, and, being emergency measures, they are usually not carefully planned and thought through. They almost always happen before the conditions are fully ripe for them to succeed. And so when they break out, there are always various people, some of whom may even have spent much of their lives thinking they would support a revolution, who when finally faced with one declare that now is not the time, that the working class isn't ready. But it's only through the process of revolution, daunting as it is, that workers can become ready.

Today we are in both a better and a worse position than socialists were one hundred years ago. The global working class is infinitely bigger, better educated, and capable of running the world. The Internet has greatly expanded the possibilities of grassroots democracy and education. At the same time, we face governments with massively increased repressive and surveillance powers, while in most places the socialist movement is far smaller and more disconnected from the working class.

The role of revolutionaries is not to create revolutions but to prepare for them. This requires having the humility to understand that mass upheavals don't come around at regular frequent intervals that can be coordinated with vacation schedules or life plans. But we also know that the next one will happen sooner than those in power claim—which is never again. What does happen more frequently—all the time in fact—are the smaller struggles that capitalism makes inevitable, picket lines and protests against police violence, high school walkouts and hunger strikes. It is in these fights that new revolutionaries are forged, and it is the goal of socialists to bring them together into effective organizations. These future socialist parties will look different from the Bolsheviks—hopefully nobody still thinks the key task is to organize the telegraph operators. What matters most is that they genuinely believe in the capacity of the working class to create a better society and seize the rare moments when that's a possibility for all their worth.

9.

What's in a Name?

I have a confession to make. You've been a terrific reader for these past eight chapters, enduring my weak metaphors and silly jokes for the noble purpose of learning more about socialism. Which only makes it harder for me to admit that I've been misleading you this whole time. Despite its title, this book isn't really an introduction to socialism. It's an introduction to just one branch on the socialist tree.

There have been all sorts of projects that have gone under the name of socialism, from tiny communes to military dictatorships to liberal capitalist democracies. What I've been describing, a revolutionary project based on the potential of the working class to overthrow capitalism and create a classless society, is more properly known as Marxism. Unfortunately, most people either haven't even heard of Marxism or associate it with a college seminar. In any case, it's not as if I could claim that this book represents all of Marxism either.

Marxists disagree (loudly) with one another over any number of subjects. Take the "Russia question," which has been as much of a touchstone for the left as the *Twilight* movies were for a generation of teenage girls, only if Edward had his henchmen stab Jacob with an ice pick and liquidate his entire family. That's what Joseph Stalin did to Leon Trotsky, who had become the leader of the forces opposed to Stalin's destruction of the Russian Revolution. For decades after the radical left was divided between "Stalinists" and "Trotskyists." As you can probably tell by now, I'm on Team Leon.

That's just one of the many points of disagreement within the Marxist and socialist movements. We are often chided for our endless arguments, which can be a valid criticism, but not coming from those inside the US two-party system who spend their own days intensely following the screaming matches between the party that wages endless war and cuts food stamps and the party that wages endless war and cuts food stamps even more. Compared to that racket, the debates among socialists are far more profound.

The problem is that the origins of many of these divisions go back to the response various socialists had to the revolutionary wave that swept across Russia, Germany, and most of Europe almost a hundred years ago. This leads some to belittle socialists for "debating ancient history," as if trying to learn from the past isn't the essence of archaeology, evolutionary biology, and many other fields of human knowledge. New activists are often more eager to organize protests than to learn about past ones, but many of them eventually learn that they aren't the first generation trying to change the world and come to identify with one or more of the distinct strains of radicalism that have come into being.

One strand of socialism is social democracy, which can be seen in its classic form today in some of the large socialist parties in Europe. A hundred years ago, these parties claimed to support the overthrow of capitalism by the working class but argued that this would occur not through revolutionary upheavals but via gradual implementation from elected governments. On this basis they opposed the Bolshevik-led revolution for being undemocratic. Over the course of the twentieth century, many of these parties won elections and had the chance to implement their lofty rhetoric of socialist transformation. In every case, they limited themselves to (at best) enacting programs of free health care and education that represented major progress but didn't challenge the overall authority of the capitalist class to run the economy based on profit. As the capitalists and social democrats learned how to coexist—and even get along—social democracy moved away from even mild reformism. Today most of these parties model themselves after the Democratic Party, which former Republican strategist Kevin Phillips once called "the world's second-most enthusiastic capitalist party."

The revolutionary socialists who supported the Russian Revolution eventually split between the Stalinist Communist parties and the far smaller Trotskyist organizations that opposed the Soviet Union's turn toward dictatorship and argued that socialism must be both revolutionary *and* democratic. As the world learned about the slave labor camps, mass executions, and other horrors of Stalinism, the revolutionary prestige of the Soviet Union faded, and the next generation found its inspiration in the wave of revolutions in China, Cuba, and the former colonial world across Africa and Asia. These revolutions reinforced the idea that radical change was possible and helped keep the United States from trying to completely dominate the globe (which has worked so well in recent years!), but since most of them had little to do with workers taking power they also pushed the concept of socialism further away from working-class democracy and toward the much more limited concepts of national independence and centralized economic planning.

By the middle of the twentieth century, socialism became defined as either mild social democracy on the one hand, or one-party "people's" dictatorships on the other. This division was—and still is—commonly expressed as socialism versus communism, which distorted the original meaning of not one word but two. Earlier socialists like Marx and Lenin had used *socialism* and *communism* almost interchangeably. In some writings, Marx and Engels used *socialism* to refer to that first period after a working-class revolution and *communism* to refer to a later classless era. But this distinction didn't stop them and other communists from going back and forth between the two words in the names of their books and organizations.[1] I tend to use *socialism* because it has a less tainted reputation in the United States, but if the next generation of kickass working-class fighters calls itself *communist*, I'll switch names in a heartbeat.

The irony of the supposed difference between "socialism" and "communism" was that both sides had more in common with each other than they did with anything Marx wrote. Both social democracy and Stalinism were a type of "socialism from above"—as Hal Draper wrote in *The Two Souls of Socialism*—in which workers would be granted their liberation by benevolent socialist leaders, whether they be elected in parliament or rolling in on Red Army tanks:

> There have always been different "kinds of socialism," and they have customarily been divided into reformist or revolutionary, peaceful or violent, democratic or authoritarian, etc. These divisions exist, but the underlying division is something else. Throughout the history of socialist movements and ideas, the fun-

---

1. One of Marx and Engels's early works was *The Communist Manifesto*. Their follow-up work was Engels's pamphlet *Socialism: Utopian and Scientific*. The Bolsheviks were first part of the Social Democratic Party. Later they changed the name to Communist to distinguish themselves from the moderates.

damental divide is between socialism-from-above and socialism-from-below.

What unites the many different forms of socialism-from-above is the conception that socialism must be handed down to the grateful masses in one form or another, by a ruling elite which is not subject to their control in fact. The heart of socialism-from-below is its view that socialism can be realized only through the self-emancipation of activized masses "from below" in a struggle to take charge of their own destiny as actors (not merely subjects) on the stage of history. "The emancipation of the working classes must be conquered by the working classes themselves"; this is the first sentence in the rules written for the First International by Marx, and this is the first principle of his life work.

Draper was part of the relatively tiny Trotskyist movement, which kept chugging along through the decades,[2] trying to maintain what it viewed as the spirit of Marxism, with the emphasis on working-class democratic self-rule. But without any major country to point to as an example of "really existing socialism" (and to fund their efforts), Trotskyists often struggled to attract more than handfuls of intellectuals. The socialists most focused on working-class self-emancipation were ironically also the ones most isolated from actual workers. Some of them coped by developing a keen sense of humor, others by becoming miserable cranks. You'll still find both at many a leftist gathering.

Stalinism, social democracy, and other forms of socialism all went into decline in the later decades of the twentieth century. But rather than helping Trotskyism, this led people around the world to

---

2. Sort of like The Little Engine That Could, except Trotskyists would have ruthlessly critiqued the mantra "I think I can, I think I can" for being wishful idealism that doesn't factor in the poor little train's material conditions.

reject socialism outright. As a result, many people looking to take on capitalism in recent years have been more influenced by anarchism, which rejects all forms of leadership and structured organization—no matter how democratic.[3] Anarchists have produced some inspiring and creative protests, but for the most part they've been unable to create durable structures that extend wider than circles of like-minded people.[4]

But the fairly dismal history of socialism in recent years begs the question: Why keep using a name that has taken on so much historical baggage? Some activists say that what we call ourselves is less important than what we are do, like supporting strikes and fighting deportations. Fair enough, but strikes and deportations have root causes in capitalism, and avoiding words like *socialism* means that we're not educating new activists about these root causes—or pointing a way forward to how we can ultimately live in a world free of all exploitation and national borders.

A related argument comes from those who don't call themselves socialist or anarchist or any other "label" that they think would restrict their uniquely individual worldview. But deciding to be a socialist or anarchist doesn't restrict your ideas. It gives them more structure, which actually helps you think for yourself in a society dominated by the ideas of capitalism. Most activists who reject all "isms" are deluding themselves that they are free thinkers when in fact they are limited thinkers, avoiding a systematic assessment of the big "ism" that shapes every aspect of our lives and thoughts.

---

3. There are some great anarchist activists who are much more flexible than this and understand the need for structure and organization. But it doesn't say much for anarchism as a theory that its most effective practitioners are the ones who reject many of its core ideas.

4. I will not make a drum circle joke. I will not make a drum circle joke . . .

There is a similar phenomenon in elections, where there are now almost as many people registered as "independent" as those in the Democratic or Republican Parties. And yet this hasn't led to any increase in political power independent from the two parties. It just means there are more people willing to go back and forth between the two lousy choices on offer.

Leftists who view themselves as political independents are almost inevitably part of a political tradition whether they know it or not: liberalism. Liberalism can encompass the opinions of a wide range of people—from immigrants' rights activists to the Democrat who has deported more people than any other president in history. That's because liberalism is a default category. You don't have to make a decision to be a liberal—that's just what anyone who isn't conservative is called. But liberalism and conservatism both start from the proposition that capitalism is the best possible system—they differ in that liberalism thinks its problems should be reformed while conservatives fear the instability that comes with any form of change. Unlike liberalism, socialism must be a conscious choice: a rejection of the idea that humanity can't do better than capitalism. That's why identifying as a socialist doesn't limit your intellectual horizons but frees them.

There are also those who argue that names actually matter a great deal, and for that reason we should come up with a new one that is less historically tainted than socialism. As with communism, I'm happy to welcome any new name that proves to work better than the old ones. I'll be the shameless old guy eager to use whatever lingo the radical kids are using these days. But until that happens, I'm not going to waste my time trying to rebrand the revolution. *Open Source Economy! Wiki-ism!*

Most ideas for renaming socialism involve innocuous terms like "real democracy" that basically try to undersell the magnitude of what it means to overturn capitalism. These efforts remind me of the approach of the reformist leader of the Socialist Party of America, Norman Thomas. "The American people," he said, "will never knowingly adopt socialism. But under the name of 'liberalism,' they will adopt every fragment of the socialist program, until one day, America will be a socialist nation, without knowing how it happened." Unfortunately, Thomas's prediction was turned on its head. Under the name of gradualism, reformist socialist parties around the world adopted every fragment of the liberal program until one day they were capitalist parties without knowing how it happened. Language does matter, and if we water down the words we use to describe our goals, eventually we'll water down our goals, too.

It's common sense among many activists that the best way to win influence is to be as broad and inclusive as possible to gain more people. But for that influence to mean anything, it is has to be based on some sharp and specific ideas that point a definite way forward. The socialism presented in this book is more far-reaching and radical than a vague alternative to capitalism. The bad news is that this socialism requires the majority class around the world to learn through its own painful struggles how to become the masters of society, which is a lot harder to accomplish than changing a few laws or even the whole government. The good news is this socialism envisions the majority class around the world learning through its own painful struggles how to become the masters of society, which will be a lot harder to undo by changing a few laws or even the whole government.

Part 4:

Further Questions
You Probably Never Asked

10.

Will Socialism Be Boring?

The year was 2081, and everybody was finally equal. They weren't only equal before God and the law. They were equal every which way. Nobody was smarter than anybody else. Nobody was better looking than anybody else. Nobody was stronger or quicker than anybody else. All this equality was due to the 211th, 212th, and 213th Amendments to the Constitution, and to the unceasing vigilance of agents of the United States Handicapper General.

Relax, this isn't going to be another "Danny imagines socialism" chapter. This is not my version of 2081 but Kurt Vonnegut's in the opening lines of his "Harrison Bergeron," a short story about a future in which everyone is the same. Attractive people are forced to wear masks, smart people have earpieces that regularly distract their thoughts with loud noises, and so on. As one would expect with Vonnegut, there are some darkly hilarious moments—such as a ballet performance in which the dancers are shackled with leg weights—but unlike most of his stories, "Harrison Bergeron" is based on a reactionary premise: equality can only be achieved by reducing the most talented down to the mediocre ranks of the masses.

Socialism has often been portrayed in science fiction in these types of gray dystopian terms, which reflect the ambivalence that many artists have toward capitalism. Artists are often repulsed by the anti-human values and commercialized culture of their society, but they are also aware that they have a unique status within it that allows them to express their creative individuality—as long as it sells. They fear that socialism would strip them of that status and reduce them to the level of mere workers, because they are unable to imagine a world that values and encourages the artistic expression of all of its members.[1]

Of course there's another reason that socialist societies are imagined to be grim and dreary: most of the societies that have called themselves socialist have been grim and dreary. Shortly after the revolutions in Eastern Europe that ended the domination of the Soviet Union, the Rolling Stones played a legendary concert in Prague in which they were welcomed as cultural heroes.[2] The catch is that this was 1990, Mick and Keith were almost fifty, and it had been years since their most recent hit, a song called "Harlem Shuffle" that is god-awful. Forget about the censored books and the bans on demonstrations. If you want to understand how boring Stalinist society was, watch the video for "Harlem Shuffle" and then think about one of the coolest cities in Europe going out of its mind with joy at the chance to see those guys.[3]

1. This is not true about all science fiction writers, as angry fans of Ursula Le Guin and China Miéville will probably remind me.

2. The Stones concert in Prague is the setting for Tom Stoppard's *Rock 'n' Roll*, a brilliant play about Stalinism from the perspective of a Czech rock fan who rejected it and a British professor who stayed with it until the bitter end.

3. Okay, it's not as bad as the prison labor camps, repressing popular revolutions in Budapest, Prague, and Poland, and giving communism a bad name for decades. But seriously, that song is appalling.

Does it really matter if socialism is boring? Perhaps it seems silly, even offensive, to be concerned about such a trivial matter compared to the horrors that capitalism inflicts all the time. Think about the dangers of increasing hurricanes and wildfires caused by climate change, the trauma of losing your home or your job, or the insecurity of not knowing if the man sitting next to you sees you as a target for date rape. We like watching movies about the end of the world or people facing adversity, but in our actual lives most of us prefer predictability and routine.

Worrying that socialism might be boring can seem like the ultimate "white people problem"—as the Internet likes to say. *Sure, it would be nice to eliminate poverty, war, and racism . . . but what if I get bored?* But it does matter, of course, because we don't want to live in a society without creativity and excitement, and also because if those things are being stifled then there must be a certain ruling clique or class that is doing the stifling—whether or not they think it's for our own good. Finally, if socialism is stale and static, it will never be able to replace capitalism, which can accurately be called many nasty things, but boring is not one of them.

Capitalism has revolutionized the world many times over in the past two hundred years and changed how we think, look, communicate, and work. Just in the past few decades, this system adapted quickly and effectively to the global wave of protests and strikes in the sixties and seventies: Unionized factories were closed and relocated to other corners of the world, the stated role of government was shifted from helping people to helping corporations help people, and finally all these changes and others as well were sold to us as what the protesters had been fighting for all along—a world in which every man, woman, and child is born with the equal right to buy as many smartphones and factory-ripped pairs of jeans as they want.

Capitalism can reinvent itself far more quickly than any previous economic order. "Conservation of the old modes of production in unaltered form," write Marx and Engels in *The Communist Manifesto*, is "the first condition of existence for all earlier industrial classes. Constant revolutionising of production, uninterrupted disturbance of all social conditions, everlasting uncertainty and agitation distinguish the [capitalist] epoch from all earlier ones." While earlier class societies desperately tried to maintain the status quo, capitalism thrives on overturning it.

The result is a world in constant motion. Yesterday's factory district is today's slum is tomorrow's hipster neighborhood. All that is solid melts into air. That's another line from the *Manifesto* and also the name of a wonderful book by Marshall Berman, who writes that to live in modern capitalism is "to find ourselves in an environment that promises us adventure, power, joy, growth, transformation of ourselves and the world—and at the same time, that threatens to destroy everything we have, everything we know, everything we are."

Yet most of our lives are far from exciting. We work for bosses who want us to be mindless drones. Even when a cool new invention comes to our workplace, we can count on it to eventually be used to make us do more work in less time, which might arouse the passions of management but will only fill our days with more drudgery. Outside of work, it's the same story. Schools see their primary role as providing "career readiness," which is an inoffensive phrase that means getting kids prepared to handle the bullshit of work. Even the few hours that are supposed to be our own are mostly spent on laundry, cooking, cleaning, checking homework, and all the other necessary tasks to get ourselves and our families ready for work the next day. Most of us only experience the excitement of capitalism as something happening somewhere else: new gadgets for rich people, wild parties for celebrities, amazing performances to watch from your couch. On the bright side, at least most of it is better than "Harlem Shuffle."

Even worse, when we do get to directly touch the excitement, it's usually because we're on the business end of it. It's our jobs being replaced by that incredible new robot, our rent becoming too expensive ever since the beautiful luxury tower was built across the street. Adding insult to injury, we are then told if we complain that we are standing in the way of progress. The sacrifice of individuals in the name of societal progress is said to be one of the horrors of socialism, a world run by faceless bureaucrats supposedly acting for the common good. But there are plenty of invisible and unelected decision makers under capitalism, from health insurance officials who don't know us but can determine whether our surgery is "necessary" to billionaire-funded foundations that declare schools they have never visited to be "failures."

Socialism also involves plenty of change, upheaval, and even chaos, but this chaos, as Hal Draper might have said, comes from below. During the Russian Revolution, the Bolshevik-led soviet government removed marriage from the control of the church one month after taking power and allowed couples to get divorced at the request of either partner. These laws dramatically changed family dynamics and women's lives, as evidenced by some of the song lyrics that became popular in rural Russian villages:

> *Time was when my husband used his fists and force.*
> *But now he is so tender. For he fears divorce.*
> *I no longer fear my husband. If we can't cooperate,*
> *I will take myself to court, and we will separate.*[4]

4. For these and other great tidbits of sex and love in revolutionary Russia, listen to Jason Yanowitz's lecture on the topic at WeAreMany.org.

Of course, divorce can be heartbreaking as well as liberating. Revolutions cast everything in a new light, from our leaders to our loved ones, which can be both exciting and excruciating. "Gigantic events," wrote Trotsky in a 1923 newspaper article, "have descended on the family in its old shape, the war and the revolution. And following them came creeping slowly the underground mole—critical thought, the conscious study and evaluation of family relations and forms of life. . . . No wonder that this process reacts in the most intimate and hence most painful way on family relationships."

In another article, Trotsky described daily experience in revolutionary Russia as "the process by which everyday life for the working masses is being broken up and formed anew." Like capitalism, these first steps toward socialism offered both the promise of creation and the threat of destruction, but with the crucial difference that the people Trotsky wrote about were playing an active role in determining how their world was changing. They were far from having complete control, especially over the mass poverty and illiteracy that the tsar and world war had bequeathed to them. But even in these miserable conditions, the years between the October revolution and Stalin's final consolidation of power demonstrated the excitement of a society in which new doors are open to the majority classes for the first time.

There was an explosion of art and culture. Cutting-edge painters and sculptors decorated the public squares of Russian cities with their futurist art. For the record, Lenin hated the futurists, but this didn't stop the government from funding their journal *Art of the Commune.* Ballets and theaters were opened up to mass audiences. Cultural groups and workers' committees came together to bring art and artistic training into factories. The filmmaker Sergei Eisenstein gained world renown for the groundbreaking technique of his movies depicting the Russian Revolution. The silly premise of "Harrison Bergeron" was refuted. Socialism didn't find talented artists to be a threat to "equality" or find a contradiction between appreciating individual artists and opening up the previously elitist art world to the masses of workers and peasants.

The possibilities of socialism that the world glimpsed in Russia for a few years was not a sterile experiment controlled by a handful of theorists but a messy and thrilling creation of tens of millions of people groping toward a different way of running society and treating one another, with all the skills, impediments, and neuroses they had acquired through living under capitalism, in the horrible circumstances of a poor war-torn country. They screwed up in all sorts of ways, but they also showed that socialism is a real possibility, not a utopian dream that doesn't fit the needs of real human beings. And the society they were pointing toward was a place where equality meant not lowering but raising the overall cultural and intellectual level of society.

In the many novels, movies, and other artistic renderings of socialism, there is little mention of rising divorce rates and heated debates about art. Most of them imagine societies without conflict, which is why they seem so creepy—including the ones intending to promote socialism.

A similar problem exists inside many protest movements today, in which some activists want to organize movements and meetings around a consensus model, which means that almost everybody present has to agree on a decision for it to get passed. Consensus can sometimes be an effective way to foster collaboration among people who don't know and trust one another, especially because most people in this supposedly democratic society have almost no experience participating in the democratic process of discussion, debate, and then a majority-rule vote.[5] When organizers view consensus not only as a temporary tactic but as a model for how society should be run, however, there is a problem. I want to live in a democratic society with conflicts and arguments, where people aren't afraid to stand up for what they believe in and don't feel pressured to soften their opinions so that, when a compromise is reached, we can pretend that we all agreed in the first place. If your case for socialism rests on the idea that people will stop getting into arguments and even occasionally acting like jerks, you should probably find another cause.

Socialism isn't going to be created, Lenin once wrote, with "abstract human material, or with human material specially prepared by us, but with the human material bequeathed to us by capitalism. True, that is no easy matter, but no other approach to this task is serious enough to warrant discussion." To be an effective socialist, it is extremely helpful to like human beings. Not humanity as a concept but real, sweaty people. In *All That Is Solid Melts into Air*, Berman tells a story about Robert Moses, the famous New York City public planner who flattened entire neighborhoods that stood in the way of the exact spots where he envisioned new highways. Moses, a friend once said, "loved the public, but not as people." He built parks, beaches, and highways for the masses to use, even as he loathed most of the working-class New Yorkers he encountered.

Loving the public but not people is also a feature of elitist socialists, whose faith rests more on five-year development plans, utopian blueprints, or winning future elections than on the wonders

---

5. In a wonderful scene in *The Take*, a documentary about factory occupations in Argentina in the 2000s, one worker explains that in the beginning people would get angry after they lost a vote in the factory committee, but that over time "we got used to winning and we got used to losing."

that hundreds of millions can achieve when they are inspired and liberated. That is why their visions for socialism are so lifeless and unimaginative. By contrast, Marx, who is often presented as an isolated intellectual, was a rowdy, argumentative, funny, passionate person who once declared that his favorite saying was the maxim: "I am a human being, I consider nothing that is human alien to me."

I find it hard to see how a world run by the majority of human beings, with all of our gloriously and infuriatingly different talents, personalities, madnesses, and passions, could possibly be boring.

11.

Is Socialism a Religion?

Socialists are denounced by some as godless heathens and by others as hucksters trying to build a new church promising workers their very own kingdom of heaven. I'll say this for our opponents: they're good at covering all their bases.

"Religion is the opium of the people." This is one of Marx's best-known quotes, and also one of the most misunderstood because it is usually taken out of context from the larger passage that gives it its beauty and depth:

> Religious suffering is, at one and the same time, the expression of real suffering and a protest against real suffering. Religion is the sigh of the oppressed creature, the heart of a heartless world, and the soul of soulless conditions. It is the opium of the people.
>
> The abolition of religion as the *illusory* happiness of the people is the demand for their *real* happiness. To call on them to give up their illusions about their condition is to call on them to give up a condition that requires illusions.

Marx was less concerned about whether people believed in

heaven than about a world that drives so many to console themselves that they'll be happier when they are dead. Most socialists have nothing to do with those atheists who mock religions and claim that they are the root of all our problems while having nothing to say about the dehumanizing conditions of capitalism that make religion necessary for so many people. I have particular contempt for those who use atheism as a liberal cover for demonizing Islam above all other religions. These hypocrites want to wage a modern-day Crusade without having to bother getting up in the morning to go to church.

If religion is defined as the way we try to understand what place our tiny insignificant lives have in the giant scary universe, then socialists don't oppose religion any more than we oppose culture, philosophy, or the other foundations of the human intellect. We don't agree with many of the explanations that organized religions put forward to explain the world, and we often find ourselves opposed to their powerful and wealthy leaders. But you could say the same thing for universities and Hollywood studios, and it doesn't mean that socialists are against movies.[1]

I am an atheist, but I would never call myself a nonbeliever. I believe in higher powers inside people that can only be activated in a society designed to bring them out. My belief in these powers is so strong that I have organized my life around them, despite the fact that I cannot prove their existence. Is my socialism a religious faith? That's a longstanding critique, most famously expressed in *The God That Failed*, a book written by disillusioned former Communist Party supporters after World War II. I'm not sure why socialism was

---

1. When I first joined a socialist group, I remember being asked by some friends if I was "still allowed to watch TV" like I had joined a monastery. The nineties, man. Stupid times.

the only god singled out by the authors for failure. What grade did the regular God get in the wake of the Nazis and the nuclear devastation of Hiroshima and Nagasaki, a C+? What had actually failed were these ex-socialists' hopes, which they and many of their generation had entrusted to political parties that thoroughly betrayed all of their ideals.

Dismissing socialism as a religious fantasy leaves you with no choice but to accept capitalism as the only rational reality, which is a problem because capitalism is real, but it certainly isn't rational. Capitalist economic theory borrows heavily from religion, replacing God with the Free Market, an invisible but omnipresent force that sometimes works in mysterious ways but should never be questioned because we live according to Its law. When economies succeed, all praise is due to the Free Market. When they fail, we must have done something to anger It, like raising the minimum wage or limiting how much factories can pollute the air. Or at least this is what we are told by the well-compensated high priests who interpret Its workings for the lay people.

Capitalist ideology is not really a religion. It doesn't tell us if we have a soul or help us to understand what happens after we die. It doesn't have a deity for us to worship, although it produces more than a few billionaire egomaniacs who think otherwise. Its ethos of ambition and selfishness is the opposite of those of traditional religions, which teach us to accept our place in society. But capitalism does provide answers to existential questions that all religions aim to address.

What is the meaning of life?

To have more tomorrow than I have today.

What is my place in the universe?

To compete against my neighbors for as much as I can gain, and let the Invisible Hand take care of the rest.

These are the central religious tenets across the world today. Of course, the older religions are still very much in force. They guide the dietary habits, daily routines, and deeply held beliefs of billions of people, but they no longer dictate the world's bigger decisions. Christian presidents and Hindu prime ministers are equally committed to the dogma of capital's everlasting growth. Unlike earlier religions, capitalism understands that it is people's labor, trade, and ideas—not their prayers—that produce our species's tremendous power and productivity.

But it also proclaims that we mortals cannot possibly grasp the complexities of the millions of economic relationships that we ourselves have created. To interfere with the Free Market in an attempt to plan and direct the economy is to commit the cardinal sin of pride, which is destined to meet a fate similar to the boy who flew too close to the sun. Belgian socialist Ernest Mandel writes that the mythology surrounding the unknowable workings of the market suggests that "humanity's insight into the laws of its own evolution [is] a fruit from which it should be forbidden to partake."

Socialism makes the bold but reasonable claim that we are capable of taking control of the structures we have created and using them to elevate cooperation over competition. This allows socialism to overcome capitalism's moral failure of relentless individualism. Socialism doesn't disregard our individuality. It adds to it while making it part of something bigger. Marx and Engels wrote in the *Manifesto* that under socialism "the free development of each becomes the condition for the free development of all." Terry Eagleton elaborates:

> In this sense, socialism does not simply reject [capitalist] liberal society, with its passionate commitment to the individual. Instead,

it builds on and completes it. In doing so, it shows how some of the contradictions of liberalism, in which your freedom may flourish only at the expense of mine, may be resolved. Only through others can we finally come into our own. This means an enrichment of individual freedom, not a diminishing of it. It is hard to think of a finer ethics. On a personal level, it is known as love.

Socialism is even less of a religion than capitalism because it doesn't offer the false comfort that some mysterious force beyond ourselves is taking care of us. But a socialist society might offer healthier answers to some of the Big Questions.

What is my place in the universe?

To contribute my individual talents and ideas along with the rest of humanity, and to also be a part of decision-making bodies that figure out how to best use these contributions.

What is the meaning of . . . Yeah, I'm not going to go there.

At its height in the early twentieth century, the socialist movement confidently spread its own version of the Christian message of "good news"—as the historian Lars Lih puts it—that it was the historic destiny of workers to overthrow capitalism and create a better world. A hundred years of failed revolutions and betrayed hopes later, it's fair to say that our predecessors might have been a tad too optimistic. We can see more clearly now that Marx and others had a tendency at times to make socialism seem inevitable and to underestimate capitalism's ability to resolve its deep crises (at the expense of workers) and evolve into different forms—including some that went by the name of socialism. We are more aware than ever that in the contest Rosa Luxemburg proclaimed between socialism and barbarism, our side is the underdog.

The danger for radicals to guard against today is not smug and passive certainty that the revolution is on its way but despair that it will never come. We live in a cynical age. From the top of society, political and business leaders with no clear plans for addressing the economic and ecological dilemmas of this decaying society content themselves with picking the remaining meat off its bones: workers' pensions, the real estate underneath public schools and post offices, and whatever remaining oil and gas they can find.

In popular culture, every good deed and honest emotion is rewarded with a thousand sarcastic tweets. The atmosphere of relentless negativity seeps into the left, where many find it easier to run down everything that their fellow activists are doing wrong than to put forward suggestions for what we can do right. Today we know that the revolution will not only be televised, it's going to be trolled real hard.

It's easy to forget that it was only 2011 when the planet's atmosphere buzzed and cracked with the electricity of the biggest global revolt since the sixties. Dictators were toppled and shaken in the Arab Spring, public squares were taken over in Spain and Greece, and the Occupy movement spread from Wall Street to cities across the world. As people rose up in 2011 they discovered each other. In the occupations of public spaces, teachers, construction workers, veterans, and immigrants came together and recognized that they were united in a common class.

In the Middle East and North Africa, where the uprisings went furthest, so too did the breaking down of old barriers. Here is a *New York Times* report from Yemen in June of that magical year:

> In the sprawling tent city outside Sana University, rival tribesmen have forsworn their vendettas to sit, eat and dance together. College students talk to Zaydi rebels from the north and discover they are not, in fact, the devils portrayed in government newspapers. Women who have spent their lives indoors

give impassioned speeches to amazed crowds. Four daily news-papers are now published in "Change Square," as it is called, and about 20 weeklies.

New lines of communication were established not just within societies but also between them. Protesters exchanged messages of solidarity—and pizza deliveries—between Wisconsin and Egypt. Organizers used Twitter, Facebook, and other social media platforms to create an alternative global media that publicized the occupiers' bravery and creativity in the face of state repression. On a more fundamental level, there was the beginning—or revival—of a worldwide conversation among ordinary people. The international ruling class has regular summits and conferences to discuss how the world should be run. 2011 provided a glimpse of how the international working class could do the same—through social media but also through the language of mass action.

The global dialogue was kicked off by Tunisians declaring that it was time to rise up against US-backed dictatorships. Egyptians responded by occupying Tahrir Square in Cairo, which spread the message to millions in Libya, Yemen, Bahrain, and Syria. Elsewhere, working people occupied the Wisconsin capitol building and public plazas across Spain and Greece, broadcasting that it was time for people beyond the Middle East to rise up. Within months, a few hundred activists in New York City took the conversation to the fortress of the worldwide enemy, branded the movement Occupy Wall Street, and gave the conversation a common vocabulary of the One Percent and the Ninety-Nine Percent.

Over the next few years, as each of these protest movements receded or was repressed, some proclaimed—whether out of joy or bitterness—that they never had a chance and that we shouldn't have fallen for their promise. Do we really think the spirit of Change

Square and Occupy is gone just because we can't see it? Seeds were planted across the globe in 2011, and we're going to need millions of socialists to feed them, protect their shoots, and make them strong enough to weather all the poison this world can pour on them.

It takes a certain degree of faith to devote yourself to a cause you can't always see—not a dogma to clutch in the face of challenging new ideas and circumstances but a confidence to keep fighting for your vision of a different world. We don't know exactly what that world will look like, or how long it will take to win it, because those answers aren't in any bibles, religious or secular. We're going to have to write that history ourselves.

Can I get an amen?

Conclusion

Five Habits of ~~Highly Effective~~ Relatively Undamaged Socialists

I'd love to give you specific advice, but, unlike Google and the National Security Agency, I don't know who or where you are. So I'll keep these brief and general.

1. Choose a side.

The most essential ingredient of socialism isn't its analysis of capitalism but its passion to fight on the side of the people. The theory only matters to the extent that it helps this fight (which it very much does). So before someone decides whether she is a socialist, she has to ask herself the more basic question: which side am I on?

As I was writing this book in summer 2014, Israel rained bombs upon Gaza and Black people rebelled against police violence in the streets of Ferguson, Missouri. In these conflicts and others, some identified with the oppressors and others with the oppressed. Then there were those, including many who call themselves liberals and leftists, who carefully criticized both sides to justify sitting on their safely neutral asses.

Don't do that. We can express disagreements with this or that strategy or ideas being used by people in resistance, but we have to clearly support them in whatever ways we can. Until the socialist movement is a lot bigger than it is at the moment, capitalism will be challenged for the most part by people who don't use socialist strategies. We can critique from the sidelines where nobody is listening except for other haters, or we can join the fight and hopefully win some more people to socialism in the process.

2. Organize with other socialists.

It used to be a commonsense idea on the left that you could accomplish more as part of an organization than as an individual. These days, many prefer to be free agents, organizing through social media and temporary coalitions, which works okay around specific issues but doesn't do much to build the forces we need to take on capitalism in the long run.

Unfortunately, after decades of setbacks, the state of most socialist organizations is pretty miserable. Many at this point are just handfuls of aging radicals who alternate between squabbling with each other and proclaiming that they are the future leaders of the revolution. Others, like the one I organize with, are much healthier but need to be much bigger and broader to have the impact we want to have. Hint hint.

3. Don't be a snob.

Becoming a socialist is an eye-opening experience. You start noticing so many aspects of the world that are unfair or just silly that you had never questioned before. Each observation makes the case for socialism that much more obvious to you, to the point that you don't understand why your coworkers and friends don't see it. This is an old problem on the left. Many wide-eyed students who went to their first anti–Vietnam War protest in 1967 thinking that the war was an honest mistake on the part of the president had by 1968 become jaded radicals who looked down on new protesters for being so naïve as to think the war was an honest mistake on the part of the president. Don't be that guy. Not only is it obnoxious, it's the worst way to build support for our side.

4. Become familiar with the Serenity Prayer.

At every meeting of Alcoholics Anonymous, people recite the following words: "God grant me the serenity to accept the things I cannot change, courage to change the things I can, and wisdom to know the difference." This is not a bad approach to the task of being a socalist, whether or not capitalism has driven you to excessive drinking. We need the boldness to stand up for our ideas in the face of a hostile capitalist society and also the patience to understand that it is not we alone but the larger working class that has the power to make those ideas a reality. We have to recognize the factors that we can currently control in order to make our numbers as large as possible in preparation for those rare historical moments we can't control when hundreds of millions of people to decide to resist.

On a related note, the only way we can get this balance somewhat right is to be able to freely debate with one another about the best way forward and not let those arguments curdle into permanent and bitter feuds.

5. "Pessimism of the intellect, optimism of the will."

I'm stealing this one (and why should I stop now?) from the Italian revolutionary Antonio Gramsci. Building a movement that realizes the potential of working people to run the world requires both the inspiration to believe that it's possible and the hard-headedness to understand just how difficult it will be. Try to stay out of the twin traps of bullshitting yourself that things aren't bleak and wallowing in self-pity as long as we still have a chance to win.

In my experience, the best way to stay on track is to keep finding reasons to laugh—at the absurdities of capitalism and at our own sometimes clumsy efforts to challenge it. When I started going to socialist events I was surprised at all the humor amid the passion and theory. I had thought socialists would frown upon lightheartedness in a time of so much darkness. *Nobody laughs until everybody gets fed!* It turns out I had things backward. The deepest laughter comes when you're among people who are well aware of how screwed up the world is and know that there's nothing better they can be doing with their lives than fighting like hell to change it.

Acknowledgments

This page is usually pretty boring for everybody except those hoping to see their name (shout-out to Chester Finkelstein in Huntsville, Alabama!), so we're going to play a game in which some of these acknowledgments are real, some are made up, and you have to guess which is which!

This book was inspired and helped by such a wide range of people—from Karl Marx to my youngest daughter Karlmarxina—that it is unfortunately impossible for me to include them all on one page.

I have to start by thanking Anthony Arnove, Dao X. Tran, Jason Farbman, and the rest of the folks at Haymarket Books who encouraged me to write this book and gave me desperately needed feedback every step of the way. Beyond the Haymarket crew, I got great feedback on earlier drafts from Amy Muldoon, Brenna Schiman, Jessica Rothenberg, Larry Dwyer, Alan Maass, and Lucy Herschel.

I am also grateful for the invaluable assistance I received from Consuela Von Singh at the Incongruous Names Institute, Shorty and Ray Ray from the Center for the Study of Informality, and Dalton Reed and Reed Dalton at the Institute for Applied Whiteness Studies.

I never would have been in a position to write this book were it not for my incredible family—both the one I was born into and the one I've helped to create with Lucy, Lila, and Nadine—and friends who have given me support, love, and a constant stream of teasing. I've also taken strength from a number of inspiring fighters I've had the privilege to work with over the years in various movements for economic and social justice.

Finally, I've learned politics, wisdom, and much more from so many people in the International Socialist Organization, of which I am a proud member. Jen Roesch in particular has been a mentor to me, even though we're the same age.

Oh, and one more thing. Special thanks to Tom Brady and Derek Jeter for entrusting me with the secrets about their rampant steroid use and dog fighting. My lips are sealed, boys.

Index